AFRICVILLE
MY HOME

BY

LESLIE CARVERY

Published by Leslie Carvery

This paperback edition published in 2016 by Leslie Carvery

All Rights Reserved of the author has been asserted.

leslie_carvery@hotmail.com

website: lesliecarverylivesbeautiful.net

facebook: facebook.com/artistlealiecarvery

This book is a work of fiction. Real family names have been used to honor the people of this town. All characters are designed from the author's imagination. Any resemblances to people dead or alive is coincidental. The aim of this book is to give a good feeling and reignite memories to those who knew Africville and to develop understanding to those who did not.

Copyeditor: Sian-Elin Flint-Freel

Design & Typesetting: Tanya Bäck

Exerts from Lady Chatterley's Lover is a novel by D. H. Lawrence, first published in 1928.

ISBN# 978-0-9949987-0-5

TO THE PEOPLE OF AFRICVILLE
WHOSE STORIES WERE
NEVER TOLD.

CHAPTER 1

Africville, 1943

The summer air in Africville was like no other place. A warm eastern breeze danced with the cool ocean. Smells of wild roses lingered with swaying seaweed. The fragrant aromas clung to the blowing clothes as they tossed violently through the air. The dirt roads were dusty and dry and the sounds of crashing waves followed the graveled path through the quiet town.

Rita Brown walked slowly up the main drag. It was a hot July morning. The heaviness of the toddler she clutched weighed her physically and her thoughts bore a heavier plight. She wanted to put him down but couldn't. Holding him a little longer mattered.

Dr. Stan Kelsie pulled his dust-covered blue Chevy over to the side of the road and leaned out the passenger window. Frank Sinatra's voice was lowered in volume as the good doctor poked his head through the window.

"Rita, can I offer you a lift?"

Rita Brown kept her eyes downcast, looking at her dirty size eights. She had on her mother's old slippers. They were a size too big and added to the discomfort of the walk.

Dr. Kelsie waited as Rita made up her mind. Looking up the road, she could barely see the turn fifty yards ahead, and she had a few miles further than that. Still silent, the doctor reached over and opened the passenger door.

"Where you going, Rita?"

"I's heading to Pa's." Her voice was soft. The child started to get agitated.

"Get in," the doctor said kindly. "I have to get some pies from Pa's anyway. I can take you."

Rita lifted the little boy in first then slowly climbed into the vehicle. Dust followed the doctor's truck as he drove slowly up the main road. Neighbors waved and addressed both young Rita and the town doctor.

Pa Carver's shop and home was at the tail end of Africville. He owned a small store run by him and his wife, Liza. Pa was known as one of the most educated men in the town. His house was one of the nicest. It was heard that he even had indoor plumbing, though this was not true. It was a house Pa had built from the ground up — on his own. His land had been awarded to his father from the King. Pa made a living selling food products and hardware. His home was third to last from the end of the main road in Africville.

Dr. Kelsie, true to his word, had indeed entered the shop and was back in his truck with two pies in hand. Rita and child remained outside on the doorstep. It was when the child began to cry that Liza made her way out. She held on to the wooden porch door as she addressed the young girl on her step.

"Rita?" Her voice was gentle. "Whatcha doing out here in this heat? You wanna bring that baby in here? I got some juice; just made a rhubarb pie," Liza's voice sang.

Rita stood her ground, still painfully clutching her son. She felt ill. Her legs started to tremble beneath her.

"Come inside, child; you need to lighten your load." Liza held the door as Rita slowly stepped into the house.

The kitchen smelled of cooked sugar and berries. Sweat ran down Rita's neck. Placing the child down on the sunflower-printed linoleum floor at her feet, she watched Liza pour a little cup of apple juice and hand it to him. The child quickly took the drink.

"You want some pie?"

Rita looked down at the boy. He played contentedly on the floor, juice staining the nice bleached shirt she'd chosen for him that morning. Liza watched the teen girl with concern.

"Is Pa home?" Rita asked abruptly.

"He is, he is just upstairs." Liza looked at the staircase.

Pa had been up late the night before but Liza sensed Rita's need to see her husband.

"I will get him." Liza quickly moved to the stairwell.

Rita had always liked Liza Carver, a local school teacher. Rita herself had her for one year. The kitchen was completely silent as Rita and the baby sat. The sounds of Pa heavy on the staircase made the girl even more skittish.

He was a large man. He entered the kitchen like a huge gust of wind.

"Miss Rita," he greeted.

Shaking, Rita jumped to her feet. "Sir!"

"What can we do for you?"

Pa was a no-nonsense man. Rita feared him and his large frame standing over her. He was as big as his wife was tiny; he was dark and she fair. They were the oddest of couples. Rita took a deep breath for courage.

"My mama...sh-sh-she said I should come here. Talk to you and the misses."

Pa and Liza stood quietly waiting for Rita to find her next drop of courage.

"This here is my boy. He is two and I...well I don't know much about caring for no baby. Mama was gonna help but she is ill now, so she say maybe...well she thought if you, sir, was...They say you and Ms. Liza can't have no babies and maybe..." Rita's voice trailed as she looked down at the baby. He just stayed put, playing with the leg of the chair.

"Who is this child's father?" Pa asked.

Rita kept her eyes down as she mumbled, "Dennis Dickson but he says no and I ain't been with no one else."

Pa looked at Liza and in their silence they made a decision.

"You want me to raise this boy...for good like my own?"

This wasn't an unusual conversation in Africville. The town had its own ways of dealing with adoptions and child keeping. It was more respected than law.

Rita nodded, afraid her voice would fail.

"Done!"

One word. A solid word. A word that sealed the most sensitive deals and negotiations. A man's promise and his solemn vow.

Hot tears escaped Rita's eyes as she bent down and kissed the top of the baby's head. Before anything else could be said, Rita jumped up and ran for the door, her skinny legs jetting like a deer in the wild. Liza caught the door before it slammed.

"Rita!" she hollered after her.

Several feet down the path, Rita stopped.

"His name, you ain't told us the child's name?"

The faintest smile touched Rita's lips. "It's Nelson." She looked at Pa and Rita Carver standing in the doorframe. "Nelson Carver," she whispered.

With her oversized slippers and skinny legs, sixteen-year-old Rita Brown took to running back down the long road.

Hope Carver was the prettiest child you would ever have laid eyes on, with her coal black eyes against her warm caramel color. She wore two perfectly manicured braids that hung straight down with no bend. The town's people all thought Hope Carver would be the talented beauty that put Africville on the map. Or maybe that was just the rumor her mother constantly told people.

Sheila and her sister, Sarah, were born on the piano, both played since they were old enough to sit up right. Shelia decided that it would be that very piano that would get her precious daughter a career and out of the slums of Africville, like her older sister, Sara, in Boston. It would be her life's commitment to get Hope a better life.

"Hope, please hurry; you will have me miss the bus," Sheila instructed.

Hope re-wrapped the knitted scarf many times around her neck before buttoning her wool coat to the top.

"I can't even see your face. You're going to break into a sweat on the bus," her mother warned.

Sheila tugged at her thirteen-year-old's tightly wrapped outerwear but Hope refused to loosen her garments. The long walk through the town to the edge of Africville from her home was 20 minutes of cold, bitter winds whipping from the ocean. The bus ride into the city was another 20 minutes. One could freeze in such temperatures.

Hope and her mother stepped onto the two o'clock city bus heading into Halifax. Already seated in the back were Dewey Byers and his fourteen-year-old son, Vincent.

"Good day, Ms. Carver and...that is young Hope, under all that, right?" Dewey teased.

Hope pulled the heavy wool from her face, giggling, "Yes, Uncle Dew. Hi Vinny!"

Vinny nodded to both of them then went back to window browsing.

"Doing a bit of city shopping?" Dewey tried to indulge Shelia in a bit of conversation, after all she had married his cousin and they were somewhat family.

Sheila, however, had no time for the likes of Dewey Byers. His life choices were not to be commended.

"I have a piano lesson to teach in the city." Her tone welcomed no response.

Dewey smiled politely and joined his son gazing through the bus window.

As Hope disembarked the bus, instantly the cold air hit her again. Sheila pulled her daughter through the narrow city streets in the south end of Halifax city.

"And you behave yourself. Mr. Driscol pays me good money to teach him; you will be invisible and on your best behavior you hear?"

"Yes Ma. Afterwards can we get a donut?" Hope displayed her adorable face.

Sheila smiled. Hope was an easy child but somehow her mother knew the worst was yet to come.

Sheila knocked on the front door. A thin, frail looking white man opened it.

"Sheila, you're late. Please meet me in the parlor."

Sheila pulled off her coat and started undoing Hope`s buttons.

"And who is this?" He dangled a narrow finger aimlessly in the air.

"This is my girl, Hope. She had to come with me to the city today, but she won`t be no trouble."

Driscol nodded and walked off again. When all her winter wear was removed Hope stood wide-eyed in the foyer. She had never seen anything like it. The house was enormous. It had white pillars and a shiny wood floor. Paintings hung all over the place.

"Mama, this house is...."

Sheila grabbed her daughter's arm, pulling her through the corridors.

"You seat yourself right there and don't move, Hope. This is only an hour-long lesson."

The violet paisley chair was beautiful. Hope hopped up into it and watched her mother uncover the beautiful black baby grand. It was the most beautiful piano Hope had ever seen. She considered touching its fine lacquer wood finish but Mr. Driscol entered the room eagerly. Taking a seat on the bench he looked up at Sheila as he clasped his hands together and stretched his long, bony fingers.

Henry Driscol banged on the keys and questioned everything Sheila explained to him. He constantly looked over to where Hope sat quietly, his beady eyes scanning her from head to toe.

"She is a pretty girl, your daughter."

Sheila smiled politely as she placed a new sheet of music in front of him. An unsettled feeling came over her.

"Does she play?" he asked, completely distracted.

"She does play," Sheila answered.

"Maybe you can sit here with me; we can play together," he addressed Hope, his fingers lightly tapping the ivory keys.

Fear flashed across Hope's face. Sheila was the first to speak.

"I don't think that is such a good idea, Mr. Driscol. Hope is going to wait out in the porch."

Shelia nodded to Hope, who obediently grabbed her clothes and headed out of the door quickly. Twenty minutes later Shelia joined her daughter in the cold porch. Pushing her out the door, they headed to the bakery.

Hope ate her jam-filled donut on the bus ride back to Africville. Hope didn't ever return to the Driscol residence. She didn't accompany her mother to any other teaching jobs.

CHAPTER 2

A few years later

Fifteen-year-old Hope Carver rushed out the back door.

"Hope Louise Carver, where you think you are going?" Sheila was always on full alert when it came to her teen daughter.

"Mama, have a C.I.G.T meeting this evening. I don't wanna be late. Sally is meeting me at the church; we learning to sew, so I can make you a pretty dress this Christmas." Hope smiled trusting she sounded sincere.

"And your piano practice?" Sheila asked.

"I already put in an hour and I promise on the weekend I plan to play a whole lot more, but my friends are waiting on me, Ma. I gotta go, Ma."

Sheila unfolded her ironing board.

"You make sure you're back here five minutes after the church meeting, Hope, I mean it. I don't want you outside in the night."

Hope squeezed passed her mother, kissing her lightly on the cheek, and headed out the front door.

"Yes, Ma."

The warm wind was at her back as she headed to the church, which was located in the center of the town. Hope passed many relatives and family friends; she declined two rides from neighbors. That was the Africville way; if you saw someone on the road you offered them a lift.

Walking quickly towards the church she saw her friend, Sally Oliver. Sally waited for Hope a few houses from the church. She stood a few inches shorter than Hope; she was a curvy teen with an uncontrollable head of hair.

"Maddy wants us to go get her at her place," Sally whispered like she was had been sworn to secrecy.

"But we are already at the church. Why didn't she just meet us here?" Hope linked arms with her friend and they walked past the little white church.

Maddy Cassidy lived in a little green wooden house, not really on the main road but not far off.

Irene Cassidy, Maddy's mom, answered the door.

"Hi girls, I hear you all going to learn to sew today?" Irene held the door for both girls to step into the dark hallway.

"Hello Mrs. Cassidy," Sally sang.

"Hi! Yes ma'am," Hope answered.

"Madeline is upstairs; go on up. Make sure Maddy pays attention. She needs all the skills she can get. She ain't pretty like you, Hope. She gonna have to work for a living." It was one of the many digs Maddy's mom often threw at Hope.

Irene took a long drag of her cigarette. Hope knew when Maddy's mom had had a drink. She looked ugly and said mean things. The girls headed up the creaky staircase.

Hope burst through the door, startling Maddy who was engrossed in her mirror, painting her face.

"Geesh, you scared me!" Maddy yelled.

Both Hope and Sally plopped down on Maddy's bed. There was nowhere else to sit in the room.

"Sorry…whoa, your mama knows you have all that slap on your face?" Hope teased.

"She gave it to me, besides it's just a little lipstick; it's called coral."

Hope rolled her eyes. "Fine, you and your coral lips are making us late. Let's go."

Sally and Maddy exchanged looks. Hope caught wind of the exchange.

"What?" she demanded.

Maddy closed her bedroom door before joining her friends on the bed. "I heard the boys are playing on the court behind Pa's store."

Hope was shaking her head before Maddy could finish.

"No, listen. Our boys are playing some guys from Hammonds Plains. All kinds of guys are coming, Hope, we don't want to miss this," she pleaded.

"Maddy, I told my ma we was going to church. She find out I lied… and well there will be no more Hope Carver."

Sally giggled. Maddy stood up and went back to her mirror, this time adding crazy rouge to her dark skin.

"And who is gonna tell her? We will only stay as long as the meet then go right back home." Maddy, pleased with her new face, looked to Hope. "I know Sally is on 'cause that skinny boy, Gerald, is playing."

Sally giggled. "Shut up! He ain't skinny...he little-boned."

All the girls laughed. Sally would always tell people she was big-boned when they commented on her weight.

"So, you in?" Maddy pleaded.

Hope nodded reluctantly.

The three teen girls crept up through the town using back roads and railway tracks. The game was on. Africville boys were shirtless and the nearby black community of Hammonds Plains wore t-shirts.

"We sit and cheer for our own," Maddy announced on arrival.

She took up a seat on the broken bench close to the home team. Hope hovered. Only a few of the community folks had come out. Pa Carver sat with his son, Nelson. Dewey Byers was there to watch his son, Vincent. Mostly men and children occupied the make-shift benches. Hope took a small relief in that.

"Foul!" Gerald Desmond, a dusty-haired boy from the Hammonds team, yelled.

"Ain't no foul! What kinda fool would call that a foul?" Andre Howe was holding the ball under his arm as he stepped much too close to the outsider.

"You call me a fool?" The Hammonds player was a big thick boy.

Andre looked back at his teammates.

"Uhhh yeah, I am." Andre Howe was one of Africville's best players.

The next thing to happen was so fast that most didn't catch the play. Teammates from the opposing team started moving in. Gerald powered a forward punch, knocking the basketball free from Andre's hug. Vincent crossed the court in record speed, placing himself directly between the two boys who now both had their chests pushed out with aggression.

"Fellas, we don't want this to be a problem now, after all, this is just a friendly game." Vincent pointed to the ball, which was quickly scooped up and tossed to him.

"Brother called a foul!"

Vincent pushed the ball into Gerald's mid-section and pushed his friend, Andre, in the opposite direction, ending the discussion.

The game resumed without incident. When it finished, Sally wasted no time crossing the court to talk to the guy she had her eye on. Maddy, too, had disappeared soon after the game ended, leaving Hope sitting by herself.

"Well now, look who came to cheer on her home team." Vincent was standing inches from Hope, covering his sweating brown skin with an old hole-ridden t-shirt.

"Hey Vin, you played a good game." Hope felt a tiny blush come on.

"Ten points; not my best, not my worst, but got my exercise." He smiled.

Vincent followed Hope's gaze and saw her friend, Maddy, talking to Andre and some of the guys.

"I am heading down the road; I'll walk ya home if you're done here?"

Again, a sneaking blush swept over Hope's face. She waved at Maddy, who nodded back. Sally was lost in conversation.

Grabbing his gear, first Vincent helped Hope down from the bleachers. It was dusk, a beautiful hour in Africville; the air was gleaming and an orange glow lit the road.

"Main road or track?" Vincent offered.

The tracks would be more secluded and less chance of Hope being caught, but she pointed to the main gravel road behind Pa's shop.

"I tend to be a bit clumsy on the tracks," Hope admitted.

"You, clumsy? Well, Hope Carver, I always pegged you for a graceful bird," Vincent teased.

"So then you didn't hear about my ice accident last wint..." Hope attempted to sway the conversation.

"I mean…" Vincent stopped walking and looked at the flushed girl before him. "Hope, I know we live in a small, I mean real small-ass town, but you can't believe everything you hear."

Hope started walking again.

"Well, I heard you were in jail last winter; is that the truth?"

Vincent pulled Hope to the side of the road. He set his gear down on the roots of an old apple tree.

"You really want to know?" Vincent grinned.

"Yeah, I wanna know." Hope eased herself behind the tree out of view of the road travelers and neighbors.

"So what you hear?" Vincent lit a cigarette.

Hope wanted to show disapproval but she secretly thought Vinny was cool when he smoked.

"Heard you were in jail last winter. But no one knows why. People just talk and stuff," she spoke up.

Removing the cigarette, Vincent smiled as smoke escaped his teeth. "I wasn't in no jail, Hope. I am 16, one year older than you. What you think they put teenage kids in jail?"

"So where were ya then?" she challenged.

Vincent liked looking at Hope; she was the prettiest girl in Africville, hell, all of Nova Scotia, he was sure of this. He took his time talking, not wanting this moment to end.

"I was in juvey...in Shelbourn County. That is where lil' niggas go when they misbehaving."

"You got caught stealing from the trains?"

"Nope."

"Smoking?"

Shaking his head, he puffed on his cigarette, clouding his image with a light haze.

"Skipping school?"

"Naw, I got sent down for the cardinal sin."

Hope waited for Vincent to release his last puff of smoke.

"Not honoring thy father. I and Dewey had us a big fight. At the end of the day he had to say whether I stay or they take me. I was 15 and he knew, like I knew, the next fight we had wasn't going to be a man and a boy." Vincent picked up his sports bag again. "Come on, Hope, it will be dark soon and your mama won't be happy her little girl is out on the roads after dark."

"Well, like you said, I am only a year younger than you, so I ain't no child either." Hope smiled, quite proud of herself.

"Well then, guess I will be walking you to your door."

"No, I mean, that won't be necessary. You can walk me to the church and that will be just fine, Vinny."

Vincent chuckled, peeking at Hope from the side. "Yes Ma'am."

A few of her church group friends had already passed her on the road. Vincent smiled.

"Well, Hope Carver, you didn't skip a church meet to go look at boys now did you?" Vincent teased when they were out of ear-range of the girls.

"I should hurry. My mama is waiting." Hope found her facing getting hot again. Vinny Byers was always teasing her.

"Isn't that your mom heading towards the church?" Vincent pointed.

It was indeed Shelia Carver carrying a round plate covered with a tea towel. Hope froze on the very spot she stood, unable to even change her facial expression.

"Hope? That you?" Shelia squinted into the dusk.

"Mama, I...I was just..."

Shelia reached the two youths.

"Vincent." Her voice dropped.

"Evening, Ms. Sheila."

"Hope, why are you stood out here? You need to get yourself home after group; you still have piano lessons to do."

"Yes ma, I was..."

"I am sorry, ma'am. I saw Hope getting out of her church group and I stopped her to ask about some school work. I was just going to offer to walk her home." Vincent was charming.

Shelia was quite skeptical but it took her only two seconds to fix those uneasy feelings.

"Well, thank you, but I have a better idea. I offered to make this for Dr. Kelsie and, well, since you're heading back up the road, why don't you take this to him and I will walk my baby girl home?"

Vincent took the casserole plate and smiled. "Sure thing, Ma'am. You have yourself a great evening and bye, Hope."

Sheila smiled and turned her daughter back towards home. They walked down the main road as the sun sank behind them.

"I don't want you keeping company with that boy, Hope, you hear me?"

"Vinny? Why?"

"I don't know, something about that boy don't sit easy with me."

"Is it 'cause his mama is a white woman from the city?" Hope knew she was stepping into a danger zone with her mother, but she felt a bit daring this evening.

"Shut your mouth, child, you don't even know what you're saying," a very indignant Sheila huffed up her front steps. "Ain't no matter, that piece, that...woman is white or blue, she would be all up here in our town shaking her tail, and the stupidest of all folks, Dewey Byers, just fell for it. He was so...anyway, she got pregnant and dropped that child off like last week's dirty laundry. She never came back. Africville raised that boy and Dewey, well, he raised the bottle. We don't have problems here with white folk, Hope. Look at Gina's husband! He straight from the Netherlands; they don't get any whiter. He lives here, respects our ways. It's our own city white folk that we need to be careful of. They ain't never brought us nothing but bad news."

Sheila opened the door and entered her house. "You get your lessons in, it's getting late."

"Yes Mama." Hope quickly moved past her mother to the piano in the parlor. She had created a mood and thought best to stay on Sheila's good side.

Hope pounded away on the piano while her father rested on the sofa. Winston pretended to be sleeping whenever Sheila entered the room. When she left he would open his eyes and wink at his daughter who played beautiful music.

CHAPTER 3

Eight-year-old Nelson Carver sat in the kitchen lacing his winter boots. He was excited because winters in Africville were adventure-filled — ice froze the harbor, the trees were bare and the view extended across town. He and his friends found many fun pastimes. Liza caught her boy just before he rushed through the back door.

"You got your hat?" Lisa asked.

"Don't like that hat." Nelson doubled his mitts, making it impossible to use his fingers.

Liza reached for the grey wool hat off the hook. "You gotta wear a hat, baby, it's way too cold out there."

Nelson made an unhappy face. His mom pushed the hat over his head, pressing on his eye lashes.

Liza turned to hear the screen door slam.

Outside Nelson ran as fast as he could. The snow drifts were deep in some areas and shallow in others. His friend, Mookie, lived six houses down the road. Mookie was already dressed in his oversized winter coat, doubled mittens and a scarf that seemed to wrap several times around his neck.

The two boys ran outside like the house was on fire. They stopped by the tracks and listened to the rails.

"Nuthin' coming." Mookie shook his head.

They ran to the cove where the thick ice crackled along the edge. A few teens were already on the ice, some with hockey sticks, others just sliding and falling. Nelson was a bit bigger than his friend. Attacking Mookie and throwing him to the ground was a common occurrence. Nelson then grabbed the back of his friend's coat and pulled the boy along the ice.

"Let go of me!" Mookie screamed and laughed at the same time.

The cool air froze their little faces into unchangeable expressions.

"I am too cold," Mookie complained.

"Me too, but I don't wanna go home yet," Nelson responded.

It was true if you went home and took off all your gear and thawed out you wouldn't want to come out again and the winter days were short as it was. The solution came to them both at the same time.

Seeking refuge, they entered Hanna's shop. Tracking boot-loads of snow, they let the warmed air loosen their faces. Hanna had a cracking wood fire warming her shop. The small store had jars of colorful candy, canned goods and buckets of dry foods. Hanna Skinner sat her big body behind the counter, listening to the radio show.

"What you boys want?" she asked, looking through the jellybean jar.

" Dunno," Nelson answered.

"We just going look for a minute," Mookie added.

"Uh huh." Hanna turned her attention back to the show, letting the boys warm their fingers on her radiator. She would mop up their puddle once they left, something she had to do all day, everyday anyhow.

The bell on the door sounded as Stan Kelsie rushed through like the cold wind on him.

"Good day, Ms. Hanna. How are you? It's a cold one!"

Hanna slowly raised herself and stood behind the counter. "Doctor," she smiled, "I's be just fine, thank you. I imagine it is."

Dr. Kelsie saw the boys turning over their mitts.

"Boys."

Nelson nodded his head extra hard while Mookie mumbled, "Sir."

"How are your supplies holding out?" He returned his attention to Hanna.

Hanna Skinner was also the town's midwife. She and Dr. Kelsie worked together and he made sure she always had some of the supplies he was privy to from the city hospital.

"Well you know Shelby is eight months and Mrs. Brown is expecting twins in six weeks or so. I could use a few things."

The good doctor nodded. "Write me up a list and I will see you get what you need."

"Thank you so much, Stan. Oh, and one more thing, could you send one of those younglings down to break my well water? It's been frozen for two days now."

"Two days, Ms. Hanna, you suppose to let someone know these things."

"I know; I just hate being a burden. Anyway what can I get you?"

"You are never a burden, my lady." He looked to the shelves. "I thought I would get today's paper, two rolls of toilet paper and, if you don't tell my wife, a large portion of your corn soup."

Hanna chuckled, reaching for the containers. "Dr. Kelsie, you come in here for soup every Saturday and you think your lovely wife doesn't know? Hell, whole town knows Debra is a horrible cook!"

Dr. Kelsie laughed, "Oh, and get these two a bag of candy too."

Nelson and Mookie grinned as they stepped to the counter and received a bag of mixed candy. Warm mittens, fingers working and candy for energy — the boys were ready for more outdoors.

After more snowballing and ice races, the boys parted ways and little Nelson ran towards the house. He reached the steps and pulled the heavy hat off his head as he stepped in. Liza was already pulling food from the oven when he entered.

"Go wash up. Food will be on the table in a few minutes."

"My hands are too cold!" the child complained.

Liza reached for the large copper kettle on the stove. "That is why I warmed the water for you. Come on now."

This pleased the boy. Often he had to wash up in cold water and had to fetch water which made him cold, but tonight was going to be a better night — warm hands and he smelled the lingering aroma of baked apples.

This hallmark moment ended when Nelson heard his father's footsteps heavy on the old wooden stairs. He walked through the kitchen with a dark cloud as he mumbled and grumbled whilst putting on his coat.

"You're not going to eat?" his wife asked.

"Nope, save me a plate. I got to go into town for a meeting."

Liza removed his plate from the table.

"I will be home around eight tonight; things might run longer. The city will once again make up excuses as to why they cannot put us on the waterline. This is getting to be exhausting traveling into the city and coming back with nothing. They can build a bridge to reach another city but can't lay pipes for folk to have running water?"

Nelson pushed the boiled potatoes around his plate.

"Ms. Hanna's water is frozen," Nelson volunteered. "When we have running water, we won't need the wells, right Pa?"

"When we have running water, you can wash your hands on your own and you won't need a pee bucket in your room, a bucket you seem to think empties itself? You are a big boy now. You need to start doing things on your own. I don't wanna see nothing more in that bucket, you hear me, boy."

Ashamed, Nelson dropped his head. "Yes sir."

Pa grabbed his hat and headed out the door. Liza pulled her pie from the oven. She knew a piece of apple pie with ice cream and a night story was going to put her little Nelson in a good mood.

CHAPTER 4

Winters were so long in Nova Scotia. The spring took forever to make its way. The frost still clung to the small village, blowing chilling air from the ocean. It was almost June before Africville experienced any retreat from the harsh winters. Most houses were heated by coal and wood furnaces. Keeping warm was always a challenge. Residents came and left the town in a cold hurry. People stayed inside. Socializing was almost nonexistent after Christmas.

However, at the first signs of spring, everyone started coming out. Neighbors caught up on life. Children took to the roads and fields, clothing and loose garments were often flung in the air. The unpaved roads were soft and muddy paths. Dogs in heat barked sad songs in the night. Spring brought life to the town.

Hanna opened her shop at 8 a.m. as she had done for 47 years. She turned her radio on and started her morning sweep of the porch. Irene Cassidy was her first customer; she often came in the afternoon to visit Hanna and talk gossip.

"I am out of bread." Irene pulled a crumpled bill from her bra.

"You staying for a coffee?" Hanna asked, knowing full well Irene had been sneaking around with Charley Mantley and he was still holed up in her bed.

"Can't this morning. Gotta make Maddy's breakfast; she got a...she going into town."

Hanna nodded her head, pretending to believe her friend. The store stayed busy throughout the day. Most folks needed eggs, canned food, cigarettes or milk. Hanna also carried some meats and, if the season was right, sometimes had some rabbits or moose meat. Fish couldn't be sold in Africville; everyone fished from the basin and some sold their catch from their trucks in the city. But everyone gave to their neighbors. Most city folk wouldn't consider eating the things from the harbor, which was fine with the Africville residents.

The sun was setting and Hanna finally had a break. She sat on her porch feeling the fresh sea breeze on her face. Hanna was born in Africville, she had never in her 66 years left the Province. Her brothers had both moved as young men but she never wanted to be anywhere else.

Irene Cassidy made her way back to the shop and she took a seat on the porch with Hanna. The sinking sun created a beautiful orange glow across the town. Both women watched as a brand new Cadillac slowly crawled up the main road.

"That's Russell's new ride; everyone been talking about it," Irene huffed.

Hanna gazed down the road. "You know, I worked this store every day for forty some years and delivered over thirty children in this very town, but I could never afford me no brand new car like that."

"All those railroad men be raking in the money, some even have houses here and in Montreal, I hear.

"Must be nice."

"Working the rails the best job a colored man can get." Irene started lighting her cigarette.

"And getting a rail man is the best man a color gal can get," Hanna smirked.

The shiny red Caddy passed them slowly as Russell Oliver waved to Irene and Hanna.

The weather got warmer, the ground harder and colors popped up everywhere. Leaves filled the trees, wild roses appeared along every path and homes were being repaired and painted. The sea wind was still a constant, but now a welcoming breath.

Ten-year-old Nelson rushed into the house, letting the screen door slam behind him. Liza and Pa were both in the store performing general store tasks.

"Boy, what I tell you about slamming my door?" Pa growled.

Nelson looked back at the door.

"Sorry." He looked to Liza who always offered a gentler word for him.

"What's your hurry anyhow?" She smiled.

"I was down by the water with Mookie and some boys and we saw some painted trucks driving up the road, with colors and things, and one of the boys, he says they Gypsies; he says they come here and steal children!"

Liza tried not to laugh but the sheer fear on her boy's face was so cute. It was true for the past few years a few Gypsy families had traveled and set up a camp in Africville. They helped build and repair houses for food and fuel. The stories about them stealing children were tales told to keep a child at bay. The tale continued to grow.

"Those people come here to live and work, they are not after children."

"Are you sure?" Nelson tucked his head under Liza's arm. He trusted every word she spoke.

"I am sure. Now you go get that wood brought in before Pa gets in and has words about it."

"Yes ma'am." Nelson grabbed two cookies from the bear cookie jar and headed out back. Liza made cookies twice a week. The jar had never been empty.

CHAPTER 5

Sweet June air and the lovely sound of a piano made for a joyous occasion. Hope sat at the piano in her Sunday best. Her mother had invited the visiting pastor for tea. Maddy and Sally also attended.

''She plays heavenly,'' Reverend Upshaw praised. What a gift! He tried to pay strict attention to this young girl's Godly gift but the bobby socks that left only inches of perfectly brown skin visible, the movement of her breast as she played the further keys and her face, so pretty and flawless… The Reverend was finding himself quite uncomfortable knowing the other teen girls were on to him. "Let's have that in the kitchen." It was the Reverend's attempt to remove all images of Hope seated at the piano. "Please keep playing," he insisted as he redirected Sheila and her tray of sweets and tea.

As soon as the adults left the room a giggling Sally and Maddy approached the piano. Maddy took a seat on the bench as Sally stood close by.

"Oh sweet angel of glory, please play us your sweet music," Maddy teased.

Hope played on until she came to the end of the piece.

"Behave yourself!" Hope scolded playfully.

"Can't you play something a little less...?"

"Heavenly!" Maddy interrupted Sally. "Something with soul and life!" Maddy was unbuttoning her blouse.

Hope smiled. She played a few bars of jukebox-type music. The girls howled in laughter.

"Yeah!" Maddy jumped up and started to move her body.

Hope banged out a few more sinful notes of blues and Maddy swayed her hips round. The three were lost in the moment dancing and moving. No one heard or had seen the horrified Sheila enter the room. Sheila slammed the cover of the piano down, just missing Hope's fingers.

"Sally, Maddy, it is time you girls made your way home now." Her tone was crisp.

Maddy found her Sunday coat and rushed towards the door with Sally in tow.

"Hope Carver, jukebox music in my house on the Lord's day, while I am entertaining the Reverend?" Sheila's 'are you crazy' face surfaced. "I can't even...why, why in the name of...why? Hope, I spend time to teach you and nurture you to have a life in music and to grow and you show nothing but disrespect to me. If that is what you want to do with your life, fine, but I will not spend another minute of my time teaching you." Before more words could exit her lips, she huffed and stormed out the room. Hope had never seen her mother in such a state. Reverend Upshaw emerged from the kitchen.

"So I will be on my way," he said.

Sheila had been so angered she had left the preacher in the kitchen.

Hope nodded.

Still early evening, Pa relaxed after a long day in his sitting room going through the daily newspaper. Liza sat opposite him with a ball of yellow yarn and knitting needles. Pa's mood started to cloud over from his normal state of grumpy to a whole lot of edgy. Collapsing the paper on his knee, his voice boomed, "White man, won't leave us be?"

Liza had overheard some of the gossip and knew things were still quite unsettled between the city council and the town of Africville.

"What now?" she asked, afraid of the answer.

"They are actually talking about putting a dump here. An infested dumping ground for the whole city, right here."

Liza stopped knitting. This was the most absurd thing she had heard.

"A dump?" The words and images were flashing through her mind when she saw Pa jump up and get his jacket. "Well, where are you going?"

"I am going to meet with the town, going to gather some folks now. Can you go get someone to open the church? Tell everyone, Liza, we need everyone there."

Liza too got to her feet and reached for her shoes.

"A dump, like we don't already take enough garbage from the white man," Pa mumbled as they headed for the door.

The church was indeed packed with residents. It was a warm summer evening but a cool breezed constantly pushed the old door back and forth. Most people brought their young ones, who stood around the front steps of the church. Rita Brown smiled at Nelson, who had been chasing one of the other children around the church. The town had been as outraged as Pa himself. Some of the women even cried. Hanna Skinner was most outraged. She kept her hand balled in a fist and people steered away when she began waving it around.

The town protested and wrote letters, they fought and complained, but the following summer, the city of Halifax did drop a rat-infested, smelly dump only a few miles from the last house in Africville as promised. The dump brought way more undesired traffic through the town. The changes in Africville had begun.

CHAPTER 6

Sister Gina and Sister Marion had been wiping down bibles and cleaning the church all morning. Everything began to look picture perfect as the May sun filled the room.

"What lessons are you doing with the girls today? "Sister Marion asked.

"Well, I was up all evening writing out a plan. I want to talk to the girls about hygiene and cleanliness and I was just thinking it's is such a perfect May day, maybe we can keep the church clean and have a session outside."

Sister Marian stopped what she was doing. "Outside?"

"Yes, sister. You yourself said it was the best spring day in a long time. We can just grab the extra chairs from the basement. Will be nice for the girls to have some fresh air."

Sixteen young girls filtered into the church in the afternoon. Gina Flemming escorted the girls all out to the front lawn. The day really was glorious. The ladies had set out chairs in a circle. With flowcharts and handouts, the Canadian Girls in Training (C.I.G.T.) meet had begun.

Hope had Sally and Maddy on either side of her. They had been facing the road. Hope was the first to see the two large city garbage trucks slowly making their way up the main street. Maddy and Sally also turned to watch. Sister Gina continued to lecture in the importance of flossing. One moment everything was quiet and relaxing, the next, 25 tons of raw metal crashed. A wild dog had run out in front of one of the trucks. The other had slammed into the back of the first. The noise was unbearable but what happened next was complete chaos for sixteen young girls and two church ladies.

Gina waited for all the girls to settle down again, hoping to continue her lecture, but the next noise was even more piercing; Sally had screamed from the top of her lungs. Everyone turned to see chubby Sally dancing around her chair and the rat that scurried from behind her. Like dominos, another scream followed by another as rats came running from out of the grass, rushing through the circles of chairs and screaming girls. Sister Marian fainted. Sister Gina left her there and ran back into the church.

It was a sore point with almost everyone in the town, everyone except Dewey Byers. Dewey thought of the dump as his own personal gold mine. He spent hours of his day rummaging through crates, trunks, envelopes and boxes. He returned home in the evening, reeking of foulness. Vincent was usually the one to have to hose his father down in the yard.

"I found three pairs of tap shoes today, son. Who throws away good tap shoes? I am going to take them down the road tomorrow. Maybe that pretty girl Hope might want a pair."

"Pop, Hope plays the piano, she don't dance!"

"Well maybe that 'cause she had no shoes!"

Dewey helped himself to a stiff drink and in that same chair he drank from he fell asleep.

Sheila could not guess who would be knocking at her door on a Saturday at 8 a.m. She was quite shocked to see the likes of Dewey Byers before her. In her housecoat and rolled hair she stood blocking entrance.

"Dew? What can I do for you?"

"No, my dear Sheila, this is about what Dew can do for you."

Dewey pressed forward into the house without invitation. Sheila noticed the old tan leather bag he toted. Her curiosity was peaked. He took a seat on the old blue velvet chair. Hope entered the living room freshly showered and dressed.

"Hi Uncle Dew!" She too looked bewildered.

"Guess you're wondering why I am here?"

Both women nodded.

"Well I have some propositions for my favorite family." Dewey began untying the knot on his bag. "Is Winston home?"

"He is still sleeping."

"Oh well, I have here…" Dewey pulled a beautiful crafted man's stopwatch out first. He handed it to Sheila for her inspection. "I only want $5 for that there."

Having both Hope and Sheila's attention, he reached again into his bag of tricks, this time retrieving a ladies pair of black tap shoes.

"Ain't no one here dance tap!" Sheila huffed.

"No matter. You can take off the taps, 'dey still good shoes. Anyway, I have two more things." Again he reached his long dark fingers into the sack, this time pulling out three perfectly bound piano music books.

Sheila tried not to appear impressed but she knew the quality and worth of the books he was holding.

"Thought you might like that, and finally something here for the princess!" He looked at Hope and handed her a beautiful silver plated hand mirror.

"Oh Uncle Dew, this sure is some fine mirror!"

"Where did you get these things, because I am not buying stolen goods?"

Dewey Byers stood up quickly. "Sheila Carver! You think I am selling stolen goods, that I am criminally minded to steal, like some petty thief?"

"So then where they from?" Shelia held the books to her nose. "Dewey Byers, you tell me you didn't get these from the dump!"

Dewey chuckled. "How about everything for $10? That is a fair!" With leather-wrapped piano books smacking him in the head, Dewey Byers headed for the door. "Eight dollars, that is as low as I am gonna go!"

Sheila grabbed his bag and stuffed the things into it. "No thank you!" She slammed the door behind him.

Sheila did buy those books from Dewey, months later.

CHAPTER 7

September was the most beautiful month in Africville. The water temperature was still warm. The air was fresh and comforting. The sun shone brightly, illuminating the colors of nature all around.

Nelson was 11-years-old. He spent his days in school and evenings working with Pa at the store.

After school, Nelson rushed home and changed his clothes. He normally met his friends at the cove if the weather was nice, or the big field for running games. Sometimes the boys even hung out at the basketball court.

On this day, Mookie persuaded him to go down to the water's edge.

"Some of the guys are building a raft. They'll let us ride for five cents!"

Nelson had a dime and knew Mookie wouldn't have any. Sometimes when Nelson worked the store, some of the customers gave him a few pennies, but Mookie never had money.

When Nelson reached the water's edge, it was true that some of the boys had made a raft. It was even bigger than Mookie had described. It could easily sit four people. But during the night the raft had incurred some damages and the other boys were still repairing vital parts.

"We can collect penny winkles?" Mookie suggested.

Nelson shrugged. The tide was out and there were lots of mussels and periwinkles. A row boat was making its way into the cove. The boys watched as Rita Brown and her husband, Joe, climbed out. Rita smiled at Nelson as she always did.

"Whatcha catch?" Mookie asked boldly.

Joe reached into the bow and pulled out his bucket. "Couple flat eye, some cod, mostly mackerel."

The boys looked impressed.

"You want one?" Joe asked

Nelson shook his head. He hated mackerel. Mookie was too afraid to actually touch a live fish so he also declined. Joe chuckled. He and Rita pulled the little boat higher up on the rocks and carried their fish home.

Mookie was about to skip a rock when something caught Nelson's attention.

"Did you see that?"

"See what?"

Nelson moved slowly to the water's edge. He squinted and moved his head with the flow of the water.

"There!" He pointed.

Mookie followed Nelson's little finger. Soon the image because visible. It was a huge lobster magnified under water. The boys got excited. Nelson had already begun removing his socks and shoes and rolling up his pants. Mookie moved a bit slower. Very slowly, Nelson waded in the cool ocean water. He stepped closer, trying not to create waves. Ripples circled his long brown legs. Mookie, still both feet on land, watched his fearless friend reach into the water, quickly grabbing the crustacean. Bringing it out of the water scared both boys. The lobster opened its claws in defense mode. Mookie screamed, Nelson lost his balance and fell backwards into the water, still holding his prize. Nelson emerged from the water, holding it above his head. All the boys had come to the edge now and were cheering on the wet boy.

Soaked and leaving the ocean's trail, Nelson and Mookie walked up the main road. Everyone who passed by commented on Nelson's catch. Hanna Skinner gave a whooping laugh at the sight of a soaked boy holding a huge lobster up high as he walked the main road like a red carpet.

At the house, Liza had already heard the news from customers about her boy's big catch. She had a large pot on the stove and warm, dry clothes ready for when he burst through the door.

The table was set beautifully. Liza even put her special lace tablecloth down. The steaming red lobster was a beautiful contrast to the dinner table.

Nelson, still excited from his adventure, took his seat and gazed at his victory. "I wasn't even a scared," he bragged. "Mookie was. I could tell!"

"Scared, not 'a scared', scared or afraid. What are they teaching you at that school?"

Nelson frowned. A scolding from Pa was always close at hand. He had hoped bringing home this prize was going to be a joy-filled meal and his dad would give him a little praise but…

"You don't take pregnant females out of the water, everyone knows that," was all Pa said during the meal.

Afterwards, Liza and Nelson had a heaping bowl of apple crisp and vanilla ice cream. He had on his favorite pj's and lay beside his mom on the sofa.

"I have to go out, Nelson. I need you to run deliveries tomorrow."

Nelson nodded. "Yes sir."

Pa stared and his wife and son for another moment then put his hat on and walked out the back door. He was never a soft and sensitive type but had to admit family-wise he was truly happy.

That night he could be heard telling his friends about the five pound lobster his son fished out of the harbor that day.

The store was quite busy on Mondays. Pa had deliveries coming in and packages going out. Even Liza put in a few hours on the cash till to help with things.

Nelson had been stocking cans of beans when Pa called him over.

"Boy, come. I have something for you to do."

Nelson placed the last two cans on the shelf and went to see what his father needed.

"I got this bag of groceries for Sheila and Winston Carver. She said she is in a lesson and to leave it on the back porch. She will pay her bill later."

Nelson nodded, taking the brown paper bag.

"And hurry up. I need you back here, don't be dillydallied around!"

With a nod, Nelson headed out the door with the paper bag tight to his chest.

He decided to take the train track route. It was quicker than the main road with all of its turns.

Positioning the parcel in his left arm, he attempted to walk the rails of the track. He knew if a train was anywhere close he would feel the vibration through his shoes. He sometimes went as many as 20 steps before losing balance and falling onto the rocks. With all his concentration, Nelson had walked one foot in front of the other for a long stretch. He had not been paying any attention to his surroundings until he heard the low growl close behind him. Stopping, he stepped down off the rail slowly.

It was one of the wild dogs he had heard stories about. These dogs were said to be fierce and vicious. The dog was all black and un-kempt. It growled viciously, waiting to see what move Nelson would make. For every step Nelson took backwards, the dog took one towards him. Shaking and terrified, Nelson did the only thing he knew. He threw the groceries at the animal and turned to run. Un-interested in the bag of cans, the dog ran too. The small legs of an 11-year-old were nothing to this animal. One leap and the dog had jumped through the air, bringing the boy down onto the rocks. Nelson screamed and kicked but the dog had already started dragging his little body into the bushes. Fearing these were his last minutes of life, Nelson moved his arms from his protected face to grab a close rock but it was too late now, the dog's breath was inches from his face. The sound didn't register. The fact that the dog was no longer in his face didn't sink in. He opened his eyes when he heard the terrible squeal of an animal in pain. He opened his eyes in time to see the large metal pipe come down against the dog's skull. The animal fell down lifeless on Nelson. It was bleeding from the head. It was dead. Nelson looked up to see Vincent Byers standing over him holding a large metal pipe. Vincent kicked the dead dog off of the shaking boy.

"You okay, little man?"

With eyes the size of quarters, Nelson remained on the ground, shaking and sweating. Vincent moved to help him then realized he was scaring the boy more, so instead he dragged the lifeless animal away and kicked the body behind a large bush. Vincent picked the cans up off the ground. The paper bag had been torn beyond use. He handed Nelson two cans and held the rest.

"Gotta be careful when you're on the tracks alone. Those dogs, well…" Vincent calmly lit a cigarette.

Nelson slowly rose to his feet. He clutched the two cans. He was still too shaken to speak.

"I'll walk you back home," Vincent offered.

Nelson shook his head. "Sh…She…Sheila's," he trembled.

"Oh, okay, well I was going that way anyhow. C'mon."

Nelson looked back towards the dead dog and then started walking quickly alongside Vincent —his new hero.

Before reaching the back porch of Sheila's house, they could hear the piano being played. Nelson, now having found his voice, spoke up.

"She wants me to just put it on the porch."

Vincent nodded, placing the four cans and the bag of flour down. Nelson placed his two cans beside the items. The two started to leave.

"What kinda service you call this?"

Both turned to see Hope reaching for the cans on her step. Vincent hopped on the porch to help her.

"Little man had a bit of an altercation getting your package here." Vinny smiled, handing Hope the last can before it fell from the porch.

"You alright?" She looked over at her little cousin.

Nelson, embarrassed by the attention, nodded and turned to start walking when a burst of laughter stopped him.

"Well I don't know who won this altercation, but I think your trousers lost!"

Vinny also laughed. Nelson spun around and felt with his hands the large rip in his pants.

"Come on inside; I can patch 'em up for ya." Hope smiled.

Nelson wanted to jump onto the porch the way he saw Vinny do but given the circumstance he thought better to walk the long way around.

Nelson sat in his undershorts with a purple towel covering his ashy legs. Vinny sat across from Hope at the kitchen table while Hope sewed. When the music stopped all three heads turned to see Sheila enter the kitchen.

"And what kind of gathering is this?" Sheila asked, entering her kitchen and pouring two glasses of lemonade.

"Nelson had an accident with one of those wild dogs. I am fixing his pants and Vinny will be walking him back to Uncle Pa's," Hope answered.

Sheila nodded before returning to the living room with her drinks. The music continued.

"Thought you missed your sewing lesson," Vinny grinned.

"I made Miss Gina some sugar cookies and she gave me my own lesson."

They laughed and made small talk as Nelson became increasing uncomfortable. Hope tossed the pants at him.

"There. Not good as new, but will do," she teased.

Nelson remained motionless with the towel secure on his lap.

"You can take 'em to the bathroom and put 'em on," she suggested.

Vincent took one look at Nelson's fear and realized his situation.

"Oh Hope, listen. I wanna ask you something, in private. Come out to the porch for a sec."

Bewildered, Hope followed Vinny outside. It took Nelson a few more minutes before he stood up. Looking around, he dropped the towel and put his pants on quickly. He then joined Hope and Vinny on the porch.

"You ready to head home?"

Nelson nodded, not looking in Hope's direction. He mumbled a thank you then started walking quickly without Vincent. Vinny winked at Hope then caught up to his little friend.

"You don't need to worry about that," Vinny said.

"What?" Nelson looked a little embarrassed and a lot confused.

"About that. It's just man stuff. Girls don't even know, don't sweat it!"

Nelson huffed, "Man stuff."

He gave a little grin. Vinny Byers thought he was a man. That brought a small comfort. It had been a crazy day and he wanted to cry as soon as he saw his mama standing outside the house. Then he remembered his cousin Vinny said he was a man.

CHAPTER 8

Church services were always overcrowded in the little Baptist church located in the center of town. Visitors from other communities enjoyed the service and the after church events. Africville had never had its own pastor; many reverends took turns visiting and doing special sermons and at other times the deacons ran the service.

Reverend Upshaw had been heading the service this warm Sunday morning. Hanna moved slowly through the seated congregation, finding her seat beside Irene Cassidy. Pa, Liza and Nelson sat in the back. Sheila watched from the organ as Dewey and Vincent found a seat near the pulpit and it didn't escape her specs when Hope flashed that hoodlum a quick smile.

Reverend Upshaw marched to his spot with eagerness and spirit.

"God be the glory," his voice boomed, startling the elders.

"Praise the Lord!" the congregation responded.

"Yes Lord, we have a full house today, thank you, Jesus."

Responses and praise filled the air.

"Well now, my brothers, my sisters, we are joyful today to be here in the town of Africville, we are joyful to congratulate Sister Gina and Charley as we welcome Ricky Flemming to our community, and we are joyful Sister Hanna had no problems in bringing that lovely gift into the world."

"Amen!"

"And we are joyful that little Nelson Carver is with us today after a horrible ordeal last week. We are grateful to Brother Vincent."

"Amen," Rita Brown said softly as her husband held her tightly.

"And we are ever so grateful that we are all here another day, to praise, to sing and to give thanks."

"Thank you, Jesus."

"And as a special treat today, we are having a song from one of our youths. Amazing is his Grace!"

Nelson disliked the church services but disliked Sunday school more, so he sat in the back row playing his own games, like 'count the hats', 'how many people wearing yellow anything', to amuse him during these stretches of boredom.

The first verse of Amazing Grace interrupted his game. With eyebrows furrowed he fought the distraction and then the voice went into the second verse and he couldn't fight it any longer. He knew that voice. Bobbing between Hanna, Skinner's big straw hat and deacon Tyne's big afro head he found an opening to see the front of the church; his eyes went the size of quarters as he saw Mookie at the front of the church singing this old church hymn and singing it well. Mookie not once looked up to see all the facial expressions his friend was displaying. At the end of the service, Nelson ducked through the many people, running through the dense crowd that didn't seem to move. He saw Mookie and his little brother already walking up the main road.

"Wait up!" he yelled as he ran towards them.

Mookie stopped and pulled his little brother off the road while they waited for Nelson to catch up.

"What was that? You was singing?"

"So?" Mookie pulled on his brother to keep stepping. "We gotta get out of our church clothes; wanna go down to the water before dinner?"

Nelson looked down at his own clothes. He nodded. "Okay, be quick. I will meet you at the tree."

"Yup." Mookie veered off the road, towards his place.

The two boys quickly changed their church wear for short pants and long sleep shirts. Mookie was already at the tree munching on a crab apple when Nelson arrived.

"The cove or the dock?" Mookie asked.

Nelson shrugged. They would have to pass all the church people again if they went to the dock.

"The cove," both agreed.

Nelson had grabbed a small stick off the rocks. "Hey Mookie, sing me a song," he teased.

"Nelson, shut up!"

Nelson continued being silly, using the stick like a mock microphone. Nelson belted out 'Amazing Grace'.

"Ya need to shut up and I mean it!"

"Or what? Ya gonna sing and dance?"

"Shut up Nelson!"

Some of the boys were already at the cove throwing rocks. Rita and Joe were already out in their rowboat fishing.

"Look Nelson, it's your mama." Mookie pointed out into the water.

"Shut up, choir boy." Nelson grabbed a few rocks.

"Well, that's what I heard anyhow, that fishing lady is your mama!"

Some of the boys began to laugh. Nelson stepped closer to his best friend.

"Stop talking shit!" he shouted.

Mookie stepped towards him. "Ain't shit! Everyone know; I heard the grown folk talk. That there is your mama!"

The two boys stood chest-to-chest, Nelson's anger evenly matched with Mookie's.

"Break it up, boys." Dr. Kelsie was walking along the cove when he came across the two fighting youths.

A frustrated and angry Nelson ran. He ran to the main road and then past the apple tree. He ran all the way home. The screen door slammed shut behind him as he entered the kitchen. Pa sat at the table, last bite short of his baloney sandwich.

"What I tell you about slamming my door?" Pa growled.

Nelson walked straight up to his father until they were face to face. Both engaged in a stare down.

"That fishing woman my mama?" Nelson asked boldly.

Pa was shocked; he momentarily lost his words.

"Well is she?" Nelson demanded.

Pa pushed his chair back and stood, leaving Nelson staring straight at his mid-section.

"Sit down, boy," Pa's voice commanded.

Nelson defiantly stood his ground. "Is she?"

Pa knew Liza was out and he feared having to have this conversation with Nelson on his own.

Sitting back down, he faced his son.

"You hungry?"

"No!"

"Sit down." He pulled a seat across from the child.

Nelson sat in front of his father.

"You referring to Ms. Rita Brown?"

Nelson nodded.

"Rita Brown is your natural mother, she brought you here and you were just a little baby. She asked us if we would take care of you and raise you and give you a name. And that is what we did. Liza been a wonderful mother to you; she loves you and treats you like her very own, so I would appreciate it if you show respect to my wife and not bring this subject up again."

Pa stood up and walked over to the cookie jar; he opened it and placed two cookies in front of Nelson.

"You got that?"

Nelson reached for the cookies and nodded.

"Didn't hear you."

"Yes sir," Nelson stammered.

A strong arm on his shoulder passed for a hug and an understanding. That was the most conversation Nelson ever had with his father.

CHAPTER 9

Vincent and his best friend Andre Howe were fixing the good doctor's truck, Andre's full body submerged under the truck while Vincent smoked cigarettes in the cab.

"I need something to catch this oil. Bring me that bucket!" Andre called from under the vehicle.

Vinny got out of the truck to retrieve the bucket. "Here, you sure you got it?"

The sound of oil draining answered the question as Andre pulled out from under the truck. Vinny offered Andre a cigarette as they both leaned up against the Dr. Kelsie's vehicle, waiting for the oil to completely drain.

"Your cousin Tommy still leaving?" Vinny asked.

Andre waited for the smoke to release from his lips. "Yeah, he leaves tomorrow. Toronto. Everyone leaving. My brother has been in Montreal three years now and loves it. He writes mama all the time."

"They say a colored man can get some work out that way." Vincent flicked his cigarette butt.

"Well, ya can't be stealing coal all your life!" Andre chuckled.

"Stealing coal!" Vincent laughed too.

"Shows what you know. This nigga got an interview on Monday, nigga going to work!" Vinny's voice boomed.

Doctor Kelsie poked his head out the window of his house. He saw the two youths lazing about and not working on his car.

"Niggas should be working on my truck!" he shouted from the window.

Both boys jumped from their perch.

"We on it, Doc!"

Andre gave his best smile and pulled the bucket of dirty oil from beneath the truck.

Monday morning both Vincent and his father, Dewey, sat at the kitchen table to enjoy a peaceful breakfast together.

"What time you work 'till?" Dewey asked over his burnt fried eggs.

"Seven. By time I get the bus home will be more like eight."

His father tapped on his bacon, reducing the burnt mass into crumbs.

"Why, you need something, Pop?"

Dewey drank his coffee and wiped his chin.

"No, but I think you should get home soon as you can then put on your best clothes." Dewey had a suspicious look on his face, a smile he kept on the inside.

"What's up, Pop? Someone coming over?"

"Someone?" Dewey laughed and coughed at the same time. "More than someone, my son. Only the greatest man known to music and I heard it from a good source. You come home, get yourself together

52

tonight. This will be a night to remember!"

This was all Dewey said before his son jumped up, kissed him on the forehead and left for work.

The buzz was passing through town like wildfire. Sheila did her best to keep the information contained but even if one person in town had heard, the news would spread from the first house to the last within an hour. The gossip train seemed to be the fastest moving thing in Africville.

The Duke was visiting Africville. His love was born and raised in the town. Sheila's Aunt Kathrine had not returned to Africville since her childhood. She remained Stateside for many years. There had been gossip about her long-standing relationship with the Duke but most didn't put much faith in the stories. It was hushed family news that they would visit the town. Sheila received a letter in the post and had kept the whole thing under her hat for weeks. But being only human, she had to brag at least once. She told a mute neighbor, thinking her secret would be safe.

The morning was one of the busiest for Sheila; she had been up since 5 a.m. cleaning. After 8 a.m. she switched to cooking. She had managed three pies, a cooked turkey, peeled and diced potatoes for a salad, made a bean salad and deviled twenty-four eggs. When finished, she realized she had no space left in her icebox to contain any more food.

"Hope, I need you to run this over to Irene's. Ask her if I can keep it in her cool box until this evening and go by Hanna's and pick me up some more eggs. Ask her if she has any space also, but don't tell them anything. Just say I'm cleaning."

"Okay." Hope took the container of deviled eggs and headed out the door.

The community seemed unnaturally quiet. When Hope arrived at Irene's door she was surprised to see Irene up, dressed and had her hair in rollers.

"Mama wants to know if you can store this for her until this evening; she is cleaning out the icebox."

Irene snatched the food with a quick "Uh huh."

Hope looked perplexed and thought to ask Ms. Cassidy another question but felt the door closing on her.

The same thing happened in Hanna's shop. She managed to get her grocery needs but was rushed out.

"I have to get to the city. I have me a hair appointment at three o'clock," Hanna revealed as she reached for her jacket and walked Hope to the door.

"You are going somewhere special tonight?" Hope teased her neighbor.

Hanna looked at young, pretty Hope for what felt like ages.

"Biggest party of the year!" Hanna said then put a 'be back in an hour' sign on her door.

Hope tried to fill her mother in on the strangeness she had witnessed in the town but Sheila was far too busy to pay mind to Hope's babbling.

"I still need to set my hair and iron my dress. Your father will be going to the train station at six o'clock. I will need you to pick up those food trays and remember, stay hushed. I don't want any unwanted visitors thinking to stop by. This is a family event." Sheila brought down the ironing board. "I want you to try on the dress Sarah sent you from Boston. Should fit by now. The pink one."

Hope nodded.

Hope's dress did fit. It was the nicest dress she had ever seen. It was a pale pink with lace trim and tapering in the back. Hope twirled in the mirror admiring her look.

Sheila meant to tell her daughter how pretty she looked and how grown up she was these days but as soon as Hope peeked from the bottom of the stairs, Sheila started with the demands.

"Your father is leaving in twenty minutes for the train station. You can go get the food from Irene's now…and the bathroom, I left my makeup out, please fix the bathroom. I have a few more things to do in the kitchen."

Hope nodded She was thrilled to be leaving the house in her new dress. Winston kissed Hope on the forehead as he stepped out the door and got into his car. Hope waved her father off. Ready to retrieve the food, she started down the front steps only to make it a few steps from the house. Irene and Hanna both stood there carrying arm loads of food silver in cased dishes wrapped in various wrappings.

Hope reached for the container of deviled eggs. The women followed on her heels.

"Well open the door girl, this food is heavy!" Hanna demanded.

Still slightly stunned, Hope opened the door. Irene stepped through like she was the guest of honor herself. Hanna followed.

Sheila stopped dead where she stood. One roller still hanging from her hair.

"Ladies." The tone was most unwelcoming. Hanna and Irene feigned any knowledge of Sheila's intimation and shoved two large containers of food into Sheila's arms.

"Oh here."

"You may wanna take that last roller out yer head?" Irene unwrapped her plastic plates of food.

Sheila was equally confused and annoyed at the intrusion. Many thoughts filled Sheila's head but none gave her the solution to how to get these women out of her kitchen. Hanna also deposited her load onto the table.

"Whew! Sure is hot. I'll just get myself a little drink of water; you go on with what you was doing." Irene had already taken a glass from the cabinet and poured herself a drink of cold water. "Now, what can we help you with?"

Sheila was not up for this game and was about to push both busy-bodies out the front door when a noise from the front lawn caught her attention. Three vehicles had pulled up outside. Two older men from the town were wheeling a giant keg. More women were all walking up and down the road, heading in the same direction, all carrying pots and pans, some still steaming. It took Hope pulling her mother back into the house and putting a stiff drink in her hand before Sheila was able to speak.

She had been so angry she didn't even notice when her husband and the honored guest arrived through the door. The reception was joyful and loud as the town all welcomed the elegant entertainer. Music played, the booze and food kept coming. A few hours into the evening even Sheila had to lose her scowl and join in the fun.

Hope had been dancing and laughing with her friends. The Carver house had been wall-to-wall packed with people. The hall was a tight squeeze to navigate through. The kitchen was completely packed and so was the front yard and back porch. It took Hope almost twenty minutes to move from the parlor to the kitchen and out into the back porch for a breath of fresh night air.

She walked down the back steps, excusing herself and climbing over people. You could still hear the music and the jubilant voices laughing and mingling.

"Pace yourself, girl; too much dancing and you will not last all night." His smooth voice came from behind a tree.

Hope heard the voice in the dark; she knew immediately, before he stepped from the shadows, to whom it belonged..

"Had to catch some fresh air, and why are you lurking in the dark?" She stepped over towards him.

Vincent flicked out his cigarette. "I need some air myself. That is a lot of people in your house!"

Hope laughed. "You telling me, and people still coming. My mama almost lost her head!" She looked back towards the house. "But this is going down as the best party in Africville!" she smiled.

"You are right about that!" He looked back at the porch

"So you going to save me a dance?" Hope asked, showing her bold side.

Vincent laughed. It was a rich and soulful laugh. His quick reaction hurt her feelings. She wanted to just leave him standing there. Vincent knew Hope had taken it wrong. He reached for her arm quickly, fearing she might flee.

"No, sorry Hope, I just...well. See, I can't dance." His voice was tender and heartfelt.

"You a bold-faced liar, Vincent Byers, cause I heard you danced with Carol Ann at the school dance!"

Vincent held his laughter this time, only showing his amusement on his face.

"Hope, that was no dancing. We...I...Well...Hey...You put a slow song on and...I can do the two-step, but that there jukebox. I don't have it." He smiled sweetly.

With raised eyebrows Hope looked directly at him. It was that moment the music was brought down to a slow groove and the loud chatter from inside voices quieted. It would appear that the guest of honor had taken over the piano. All the chatter and laughter had stopped and only the beautiful sounds of a sweet piano melody played through the air. Even the people outside stopped talking; the animals were quiet too.

Vincent pulled Hope gently into his arms, surprising her. He whispered in her ear, "This is our dance." The famous two-step.

Hope felt his body against hers, her pretty dress blowing in the breeze, his cologne tickling her nose. He kept the beat steady as promised, holding her close. It was a perfect two-step, his breath on the back of her neck. They remained in the shadows, hidden from everything.

Vincent had thought to kiss Hope when the last note was played. It would be the perfect end to the perfect moment. However, this is not what happened. Just before the song ended, Sheila came out onto the porch.

"Hope!" Her voice rose above the music. "Hope?" she shouted again.

Releasing herself, Hope jumped and separated herself from Vincent.

"Here Mama!" Hope called out.

Sheila squinted to see where Hope's voice was coming from.

"What are you doing out here?"

"I just needed some air, Mama. Coming now!" Hope replied.

Hope prayed that Vinny would stay hidden in the shadows, but when she reached the steps she looked back to see the red glow on his face as he lit another cigarette.

"Who is that? That you, Vincent?" Sheila peered into the night.

Vincent took a pull from his cigarette.

"Good evening, Miss Sheila. Mighty fine party."

Sheila nodded and mumbled as she pushed Hope back into the hot, crowded house. The party went on until 5 a.m. People slept on the porch, continued to drink in cars parked all over the neighbourhood. Small groups of party-goers walked home in drunken stupor as the sun came up in Africville.

CHAPTER 10

It was the last C.I.G.T. meeting. All the girls grabbed chairs and formed small groups to begin the gossip and share stories of all that was going on in the town. Hope, Sally and Maddy stood by the altar discussing their upcoming prom.

"Mama says there is a lady in town making mine; it's yellow, with chiffon and lace sleeves," Maddy bragged.

Sally wrinkled her nose. "My mama says dark-skinned girls need to run fast and far from yellow; you will look like a shop Easter egg."

Maddy reached out quickly and tugged Sally's braid.

"Ouch!"

"Will you two stop?" Hope pushed Maddy and Sally apart.

"Stop being so silly! My Auntie Sara is sending a dress from the States. It's lavender!"

"Eeeww!" the girls teased.

It was the loud talk a few feet from the girls that interrupted them. Carol Ann Izzart was bragging about her dress and her date.

"It's pink chiffon with a big poof in the front, and Vinny is wearing a suit. We gonna strut in there like those movie people."

"Well you best be cute then, cause you will be standing up against the gym wall all night cause Vinny Byers gots no moves!" Carol Ann's friend Buffy teased.

All the girls laughed except Carol Ann.

"You know, he might not be the best dancer, but he got moves okay, and after the dance, we gonna get to those moves."

The girls all fell silent when Sister Gina entered the room. Hope looked over at Carol Ann with her nose wrinkled. Carol Ann returned the look with a smirk.

Hope's dress arrived while she was still at school. Sheila unwrapped the pretty tissue and pulled the dress from its box — lavender lace and a beautiful daisy pattern. Sheila spread the dress across Hope's bed. She took a moment to admire its beauty and sighed. In one week her lovely daughter would wear that to her first formal school dance. Sheila felt a tiny tug at her heart as she left Hope's room.

Hope's father, Winston Carver, opened the door. He faced the young man from the city, Tyrone Simmons. Hope had agreed to attend the function with Tyrone as a favor to her mother's friend. Tyrone was handsome. A small mustache outlined his lips. He had intense eyes and a chocolate complexion.

His voice was deep and confident as he introduced himself and entered the house. Winston noted the boy must be a few years older than Hope.

"That your car out there?" Winston referred to the shiny cherry-red Desoto.

"That's my pop's car. I have two important things to be careful with tonight, sir."

Winston smiled, nodding his head.

"I'll see what's keeping my daughter." At the foot of the staircase Winston hollered up, "Hope, your date is here."

"Be right down, Daddy."

Hope descended in her beautiful lavender party dress, her mother close behind her. Both Winston and the young man stood in awe. She was a real vision.

"Hi." Hope extended her hand to the young man.

Tyrone Simmons held it longer than needed as he tried to take his eyes off Hope's pretty face. Sure his mama had gone on and on about how pretty Hope Carver was but he didn't think anyone could be that beautiful.

"Well you two have a wonderful night," Sheila said, breaking the spell.

"Hope is to be home by midnight, no later, young man," Winston added.

Tyrone nodded, afraid his confident voice might have left him. He guided his beautiful date out the door and to his car. Opening the heavy car door he helped her in. This was going to be a great night; he smiled as he jumped in the driver seat.

"I don't much like driving in the city, so I am gonna go slow. That okay with you?"

Hope nodded as she gave directions to the school.

The dance was everything Hope had dreamed it would be: a gym decorated with fancy visuals, a top notch band playing the most popular songs. She, Maddy and Sally were ecstatic all night. Hope noticed that Carol Ann was there but there was no sign of Vinny anywhere. The girls exchanged gossip about dresses and dates. They made plans to meet at the shop and have a milkshake before heading back to Africville.

Tyrone had other plans.

"I don't really want to go. I wanna just return to your place, we can get a soda on the way."

Hope was disappointed; she knew her friends would be expecting her but she stayed with her date. Tyrone bought them a cherry coke and then headed his fancy car back in the direction of Africville.

"So you didn't have a great time? "Hope asked.

"I did."

"But, it's still early. Why you taking me home early?" She tried to keep the disappointment out of her voice.

"Oh no, not home. I thought we could just be alone for a bit. I was just going to pull the car up the road and we could sit and talk for a bit. I just wanted some time alone; you were all over the place at the dance and we didn't get to talk much."

"Oh," Hope whispered.

Tyrone parked his car at the very end of Africville, tucked behind some trees in the shadows. He cut the engine, leaving them in darkness and sitting in silence.

"Hope, you were the prettiest girl at the dance."

Hope smiled, feeling a hot blush rise on her face.

"And I had to share you all night, but...now I want you and me time."

Tyrone pushed her seat back until Hope was practically lying down.

"Wait!" she protested.

"It's okay, no one can see us."

Tyrone ran his hand up Hope's leg, beyond under the soft lace trim.

"No!" Hope shouted.

She first heard the loud crack as his open hand slapped her face, then she felt the heat boil from her face into her core. Hope screamed in his face. Undeterred, Tyrone leaped from his seat onto her body; he covered her mouth with one hand, holding her arm down with the other. He assumed she somehow had released the car door which flew open but it wasn't until his body was lifted that he saw she was still in the seat. He also felt the punch that landed on his jaw before he even saw the man.

Vincent had heard the sound of the car when it passed his home and a curiosity propelled him to check it out. When he heard Hope scream he moved with a force. Pulling the man out the car, Vincent slammed Tyrone onto the hood, where he continued to land punches from which no one could recover. It was Hope's screams and pleas to stop that brought him from this violent trance. When he released Tyrone, Hope watched as her date tried to stand up but stumbled onto the ground.

"No, no, leave him!"

She pulled Vincent away then looked back to see Tyrone stumble back into his car. The whole scene had left her quite shaken.

Hope walked in silence down the road towards Vinny's. They had reached his porch before either of them said a word.

"No one's home." He opened the door and Hope walked in.

Vinny ran down the hall, grabbed a cool wet cloth from the kitchen and handed it to her. Hope lightly touched the burning red mark on her face.

"Is it bad?" she asked.

Vinny stepped closer and moved her hand gently away from her cheek; a red burned through her honey skin.

"Who is he? I ain't finished with him!" he barked.

Vincent's anger shocked Hope. He walked quickly to the window. Hope feared he was going to run back out. She crossed the room, pulled him to the sofa and sat next to him.

"He ain't nobody. He ain't worth it. Just some city turkey my mama asked me to go to the dance with."

"Humph!" Vinny pulled a packet of cigarettes from his pocket.

"I thought you were going to the dance?" she asked meekly.

"I told Carol Ann I had to work late, but truth is, well you already know. I am not one for dancing. I am not one for Carol Ann either."

Hope almost smiled, remembering their special dance moment, but it hurt to smile.

Vincent lit his cigarette and stared at Hope sitting peacefully on the sofa with her pretty dress ripped.

"Hope?"

She looked up at him with her brown eyes wide open.

"What?"

"Never mind."

"What, Vinny?"

"Nothing. I will take you home when you're ready."

Hope looked to the floor. She fiddled with the rip in the dress.

"Okay." She stood, placing the cloth on the table. "I am ready."

Vinny's face was tense and Hope couldn't read him. Was he mad at her? Did he think she was stupid for going out with a stranger? Feeling ashamed and defeated she headed for his door. Vinny grabbed his cigarettes and key and followed her out.

Some of the teens were getting back and driving along the main road. When a car approached, Vinny pulled Hope off the road and behind a tree.

"Thanks." Her voice was soft.

The lights from the passing car had disappeared.

"C'mon." Vinny grabbed her arm and they headed down the road.

They walked in silence. Hope stopped several houses before her own.

"This is fine."

Vinny looked towards her house. The light was on. They were waiting up for her.

"You sure?" he asked.

She nodded, reached over and kissed him quickly on the cheek, and then she was off. Vinny stood there watching until she entered the house. Lighting a cigarette, he headed back home.

CHAPTER 11

The Africville church was filled with concerned residents. The city officials had been called in. This meeting was one of many fights between the City of Halifax and the town of Africville or, as some might say, Black vs. White or Good vs. Evil.

A nicely dressed Fletcher Byers was first up at the podium. At sixty-two years old, he still worked as a porter for the train company.

"Ladies, gentlemen, could I have your attention?"

The noise levels dropped as the residents gave their neighbor full attention.

"Now we all know why we are gathered here this evening. We, the citizens of Africville, have once again appealed to the city to request that they add us on to their water supply. Now, like most folk here, my father and grandfather owned and occupied this here land for quite some time. We pay city taxes, we care for our community, we ask very little from the city as Africville is quite self-sufficient, however basic needs like indoor plumbing and clean cooking water, well, now that shouldn't be a luxury only for white folks in the city. The City is happy to give us things we don't want."

The crowd erupted, leaving the City official in a not-so-friendly room.

"They gave us the city's most undesired: a prison, an abattoir leaking blood and discarded remains and let's not forget that wonderful gift of a rat-infested dump, right smack in the middle of our community."

The natives responded with a burst of discontentment and anger.

Donald Greenberg slowly made his way to the podium to begin damage control before everything got too out of hand. Greenberg had worked as the mayor's right hand for the past two years. He was well-versed on the complaints and issues of the town and knew more than anybody in the room that none of these issues were going to be solved anytime soon. His job was to calm the town folks down and promise nothing.

"Good evening, residents of Africville. My name is Don Greenberg. Many of you know me. I have been here many times, have brought men down here to survey the land and look to build a proper pipeline for your water needs. I have to be honest here, folks, it doesn't look good. We have found the ground here where the town is built is not solid, perhaps due to being so close to the ocean. The pipe would not be able to hold here. We have exhausted every option and we couldn't find an affordable option at all. The City wants to have you up and running like the rest of the city. We would be happy to see that happen here but, like I mentioned, due to monetary restraints and no proper landscaping, we are unable to meet with your needs at this time. We are, however, looking into ways..."

The restlessness of the crowd spoke volumes. Hanna Skinner got up from her seat and walked out. Several other women followed.

"Again, so sorry." Donald Greenberg replaced the microphone and walked back to his colleagues, who thought it best to leave the town immediately.

A warm Saturday afternoon, Sheila sat at her piano while her husband rested on the sofa. Winston was seconds away from a comfy nap when Sheila's voice intruded.

"Did you hear a word I said?"

Startled, he looked over at his wife.

"You were talking about Hope," he guessed correctly.

"Yeah, and like I was saying, every time I turn around that boy is around her. I don't like it. He just…no, I don't like it!"

"Ain't nothing wrong with Vincent, he is an okay boy."

"Okay? He needs to be better than okay to be anywhere around my daughter, and I am surprised you don't feel the same."

"Sheila, you're getting all in a huff for nothing."

Winston hoped that a roll-over might be indication that the conversation was ended but Sheila continued to talk until the sound of snoring was heard.

Hope was out the house early the following morning. She had managed to sneak in the night before without being seen. The mark on her face was less visible and when asked if she had a good time she nodded before heading out the front door. She had stashed her destroyed dress at the bottom of her closet.

The morning was already warm and the sun was just creeping over the front porches. Hope stepped up the rickety, uneven stairs. The front door was already slightly open and she could smell burned bacon and cooking grease. Hope gave it a light tap. Dewey was wearing only a tattered robe when he peaked to see who was at his door.

"Sorry Uncle Dew, is Vinny around?"

Dew was confused but happy to see Hope Carver at his door.

"No, he ain't here, he left early got some work down the ship yard. Why you looking for Vincent, Hope? He do anything?" Dew asked, concerned.

"No, Uncle Dew, he just helped me with something. I just wanted to say thanks, that's all. "

"Oh, good. Well, he be home tonight. He works in the day and I have a night shift, so I don't see much of 'im.'"

"Oh, well then maybe I will look for him a little later. Thanks."

"Wait, Hope." Dew secured his robe and moved towards a bag on the floor. "I found these here." He reached in the big bag and pulled out a little satin sack. Opening his hand he poured out two gold earrings with a pearl tip.

"Oh Uncle Dew, those are beautiful."

"Yeah, you like em?"

"I do, but I don't have any money. I am still paying mama back for my dress."

"Hope Carver, you hurting me; no one asked you for any money! " He quickly dropped them back in the sac.

"Sorry Uncle Dew, I thought…"

"I found two pairs and I sold one pair in the city for a nice price, so these here, these are a gift for a pretty young girl who makes me smile. Consider it your graduation gift." He placed the sac in Hope's palm.

Hope thanked Dewey with a hug and left him to his morning drink. Dew opened the porch door before she made it down the steps.

"If you do see my son tonight, tell him I got him a new pair of boots for work."

Hope grinned.

"Yes sir!" She turned and headed back up the road with her little pink satchel containing her secret.

Hope's next stop was at her friend Maddy's. She didn't want any of her friends knowing what a catastrophe her date had been in the end and she wasn't prepared to tell them about Vinny saving her either. She decided to tell the girls her date was boring and drove her home early if anyone asked.

To Hope's surprise it was Irene, Maddy's mom, who was the first to inquire about Hope's date from the city.

"So did you enjoy your night with that boy?" Irene was on her front porch when Hope arrived.

"He was ok." Hope felt bad lying to an adult.

"He sure did have a fancy car."

"It was alright," Hope mumbled.

"You can do better than that city slicker. I heard things about that boy and his wild ways. Guess as long as you alright."

"Is Maddy awake yet?"

"She cleaning her room. You can help or not but she ain't coming down til it's done."

Hope squeezed past Maddy's mom and headed upstairs. Taking the steps two at a time, Hope burst through Maddy's room.

"Why ya always gotta rush in here scaring me?" Maddy jumped. "Why you always doing sneaky things?"

The two looked at each other then burst into laughter. Maddy threw her book on the bed. Hope jumped onto the bed grabbing it.

"Lady Chatterly's lover — well now crazy Maddy is reading some real smut!"

"Yeah, well if it wasn't for that smut, I might not have had such a good night last night!"

Shocked, Hope threw the book at Maddy. "You vixen, you went all the way last night with Jamesy?"

"Well didn't you wonder why we didn't meet up with you and Sally?"

Hope was silent.

"Wait a minute? You didn't know I didn't show because you didn't show either! You and that city slicker took off on your own! Vixen is, vixen does."

Maddy plopped her frame down on the bed beside Hope.

"You got some 'splaining to do."

Hope didn't have the time or energy for stories or creating a scenario. She furrowed her eyebrows with the night replaying in her mind.

"He was a jack ass!" she blurted.

Maddy laughed. "Kinda figured that."

"So, tell me about you and Jamesy and the smut you reenacted from your book," Hope teased.

"Wasn't like that. Ha, I wished, just you know...if I didn't read this stuff, I don't know. I think it is romantic when you like a guy and he wants you and everything, but it is never like the books you know. Maybe black guys don't talk to women like that, you know...not like in the moving pictures or the books. They say stupid things like...'girl you make me hot, let me touch your titty'."

Hope cracked up.

"No for real, like, here lemme read this." Maddy opened the book to a marked page. She read, "...put his coat and waist coat over them, and she had to lie down there, under the boughs of the tree, like an animal, while he waited, standing there in his shirt and breeches, watching her with haunted eyes. But still he was provident — he made her lie properly, properly. Yet he broke the band of her underclothes, for she did not help him, only lay inert. He too had bared the front part of his body, and she felt the naked flesh against her as he came in to.."

Hope squealed.

"Wait, gets better." Maddy finds her place again and continues, "he is still, inside her, turgid there and quivering. Then as he begun to move in the sudden helplessness orgasm, there awoke in her new strange thrills ripping her inside her…" Maddy dropped the book. "See, Hope, that there is how it 'spose to be."

"Well, I think it could be like that."

"Then I gotta stop spending time with bozos like Jamesy. Maybe I should look for a nice city guy."

"They ain't all that either," Hope sighed. "Wanna go see a picture? I have some money left," Hope suggested. "Sure I think we can get a drive into the city. You clean your room, I will go ask my dad." Hope smiled as she put Maddy's book back on the dresser.

Nelson and Mookie had been working on the raft for a week. It was four feet wide and eight feet long. They had re-enforced the rope and even managed to connect floatation jugs on each corner. The boys were impressed with a job well done. They took turns testing it out. Nelson would hold on to the long thick rope and slowly Mookie would float out into the harbor. Soon other kids begged to be given a ride.

Nelson and Mookie stayed out in the water the whole day pulling the raft in and out, letting kids feel the freedom of moving through the water. It was getting dark when they used all their remaining strength to haul the raft out of the water and secure it on the rocks. Nelson tied the rope several times around the largest rock he could find.

"Will be fine 'till tomorrow. We can come down after church."

Mookie nodded. Walking up the main road they watched Hope and Maddy ahead of them. The girls linked arms as they walked and giggled like girls do.

The sun was disappearing as Hope and Maddy returned from the theatre. Hope's father drove them there and the city bus dropped them off outside of the town.

"Come sleep at my house?" Maddy suggested.

Still not wanting to answer questions from her parents, Hope nodded.

"I'll ask Mama. You want me to bring anything?"

Maddy shook her head.

"Just call me if you can't come."

"Okay."

Hope took a short path off the road as she waved to Maddy.

"See you soon."

"Hope, you were not home all day, now you wanna spend the night at Maddy's?" Sheila complained.

"I know, Ma, but we had a great day. We just wanna start the summer off and kick back now that school is done. We need to talk about what we going to do with our life," Hope urged.

"Well, after summer, I do hope you will consider going to Boston and take the opportunity you have been offered."

"Yes Mama. Actually, it's Maddy that needs some direction, so we are looking into options for her."

"I see. Well fine if Irene is okay with it. Just make sure you're back here early tomorrow to get ready for church."

"Yes Ma." Hope kissed her mother then ran to her room to grab a few things.

Her intention was to head straight to Maddy's but, just then, Hope caught sight of Vinny walking up the road with his work clothes hanging from his bag. He was walking so slowly. She quietly followed behind him making sure not to kick any rocks or bring attention to herself. Vincent lived in the very last house on the road. He had heard the small footsteps behind him and had caught a glimpse of Hope sneaking behind him from a car window re fection. When his foot hit the first step of the wooden porch he stopped. With his body still facing the house, Vincent spoke in a loud voice, "Can be kinda dangerous sneaking up on a brother this time of night."

A tree branch cracked under Hope's foot giving her location away. Vincent turned around smiling in her direction. Hope could make out his silhouette and that mischievous grin. She emerged from the shadows and headed towards him.

"Why is little Hope Carver sneaking around the roads of Africville this evening?"

Vincent took a seat on his top step. Hope took a seat at his side.

"I was looking for you," she admitted.

"Uh oh, what I do now?"

Hope laughed.

"Well you saved my life, didn't you?" she teased.

"Maybe not your life, but definitely your virginity." Vincent smirked.

Hope was shocked then laughed.

"Ok, so you think I owe you my virginity?"

"Well, I was thinking and do believe I been thinking about this all day. I was thinking...if little Hope Carver finds herself outside my house some late night, I wouldn't take her whole virginity."

Now they both burst into laughter.

"I thought maybe just a kiss." Vincent's voice was almost a whisper and Hope's laughter died in her throat.

She felt quite flushed, more than usual when she was in his presence.

"I can do that," she said softly. Her voice had lost its volume too.

Vincent moved in slowly and stopped when his face was just a few inches from Hope's. He could feel her breath and a nervous quiver from her body. She filled the distance, pressing her lips against his.

Hope liked Vinny a lot and this moment was one she didn't want to rush. The kiss was long and tender.

It was Vincent who pulled away first. He knew the information he needed. He knew now that what he had hoped for was true. He stood up, helping her to her feet. Hope stepped up to the top step and stood face to face with him. The warm breeze blew her hair.

"Let's go for a walk," he insisted.

Vincent tossed his bag onto the porch and took Hope by the hand. This pleased her.

Hope and Vinny walked along the road, through the paths over the rocks until they came to the shore. The sound of incoming waves crashed against the rocks. It was a warm night. The stars were bright in the sky and the tide was in.

"Night cruise?" Vinny asked.

Hope looked at him strangely, not understanding his weird question. Vincent started tugging some driftwood from the rocks. Hope soon could see it was a massive piece of something then she caught a glimpse of the floatation jugs.

"It's a raft; the kids made it."

Vincent pulled and dragged the massive wreck to the water's edge, which was much closer than when the boys stashed it.

"My lady." He held his hand out while securing the rope.

Hope was instantly reminded of Maddy's book characters. She couldn't stop smiling.

"You think I am getting on that? What if we fall off?"

Vincent looked at the raft then back to her.

"Then I will have to save you again," he said as he smiled.

Hope also smiled at the thought. She slowly climbed over the rocks to join him. Vinny helped her onto the raft. The motion was gentle. He boarded carefully and took a seat in the center beside her.

"You cold?" he asked.

She shook her head but her body language could not lie. Putting his jacket around her shoulders, Vinny wrapped his arms around her shivering body. He kissed Hope again. Laying her down, he warmed her shaking body with his own. The raft rocked back and forth with the rhythm of the tide.

Maddy assumed Hope had changed her mind and forgot to call. She continued to read her book alone in her room.

The sun peeked across the basin as early as five in the morning. It was Rita and her husband that arrived first on the scene. Joe got back into his truck and quickly sped up the road, returning in record time with Sheila in the passenger seat.

"What is it?" Sheila was miffed at being dragged out of her house so early. She had no idea where Joe was taking her but he didn't seem distressed so she relaxed at the inconvenience.

The three stood on the edge of the cliff looking down into the water below. The tide had gone out and the raft floated about 15 feet from the shore. Sleeping peacefully was Hope, with her dress high around her bare legs, and Vincent Byers, his body covering most of hers. They looked a picture of tranquility bobbing up and down as the sun bathed them in the early morning light.

The noise was not human; the sound and volume of Sheila's scream could be heard across the town. Both Vincent and Hope jumped out of their sleepy serenity. Hope's eyes flashed to the location of the piercing sound coming from the banks, seeing her mother standing there screaming. Hope forgot where she was. She jumped up, rocking the raft. Both she and Vincent toppled into the water. The screaming continued as they thrashed in the water.

It was quite a sight. Rita Brown and her husband stood on the bank laughing until they fell on the ground. Sheila Carver screamed out every sound her body could muster as Hope and Vinny flopped wildly in the water. The scene would make for one of the funniest moments in the town and definitely was the fastest growing gossip to spread from 5 a.m. till the sun went down. The town whispered how Vincent Byers and Hope Carver were caught, indecently drifting out to sea.

All day long, gossiping women found ways to bring up the latest news, each adding a new twist to the story. Hanna sold a lot more merchandise when the town had a bit of gossip.

"It's the boy I am concerned about!" Irene took a pull of her cigarettes before continuing, "I heard Sheila threatened to charge him with rape."

"Well everyone knows that girl was sniffing for trouble anyhow," Irene's neighbor added.

"Can't believe she had him put in the colored home." Irene shook her head.

Hanna took a seat. "Well, they can only keep him till he is 18 so he will be in another couple of months. That poor young man. Seems like everything is against him and he really is a good kid."

"Well I don't think..."

All conversation ceased as Winston Carver entered the shop.

"Ladies," he greeted.

"Hello Winston."

"Good morning."

"Hello," Hanna huffed as she got back behind the counter. "Will that be all?" She pointed to the milk bottle.

Winston nodded.

It would be usual for Hanna to ask after the family, but with all the ears perked, she bagged his milk and gave him his change.

"Have a good day," she said as she herded the women out of her shop.

CHAPTER 12

Nelson had received a brand new baseball for his birthday. He and Mookie went to the field for a catch and throw. Nelson had already grown about three inches taller than Mookie over the summer. Mookie had gained weight and they began to look like an odd couple of friends.

Both boys stopped talking and throwing as they watched the large stranger approach them. When he reached the boys both Nelson and Mookie looked up at the biggest negro they had ever seen.

"You boys know where I can find the bar in this town?" His voice was loud and thunderous.

Mookie went quiet and just stared. Nelson pointed.

"Follow that road to the apple tree, then take the path. It's Sam's bar."

The stranger reached into his pocket and pulled out some bills; most of them were different from the money the boys were used to seeing but he handed Nelson a ten dollar bill.

"I am going on down to this Sam's. You boys grab me some tobacco, the good stuff, and bring it to me."

Nelson enclosed the money safely in his hand.

"Yes sir! The store ain't far. We will go get that for ya!"

The man nodded and started in the direction he was told. He resembled a giant as he walked away. The boys jetted off towards Hanna's shop as fast as they could move.

Having sent gossiping women out of her shop, Hanna was relieved when she saw Mookie and Nelson heading up her steps.

"What can I get you boys?"

"I'mma need some tobacco and the good stuff!" Nelson made his order.

Hanna didn't raise both eyebrows often but this time she was completely caught off guard.

"The good stuff, huh?" she chuckled.

"Well the good stuff cost money!" She reached high up on counter and brought a rusty old tin down.

Nelson spread the American ten dollar bill on the counter causing Hanna to make another brow movement.

"Who is this for?"

Nelson shrugged.

"The giant stranger. He at Sam's now waiting for his tobacco!" Mookie gave the only information he had.

Hanna nodded as if she knew what they were talking about, but two minutes after Nelson and Mookie were out the door, she was certain she knew.

Fletcher Oliver came rushing in.

"Miss Hanna, you ain't never gonna guess who is at Sam's bar this very moment. None other than the greatest heavyweight known to boxing, Joe Lewis himself!"

Fletcher grabbed himself a pack of vignettes and some candy and rushed back out. Well at least the gossip wheels will have changed, Hanna thought to herself.

Mookie and Nelson promptly brought the tobacco to the famous stranger and were rewarded with a two dollar bill each. They left the bar gloating and talking about their famous American bill.

"I ain't spending mine," Nelson claimed, shoving it in his pocket.

The town was quiet again. Hope didn't leave the house much and Maddy and Sally were rarely invited in when they came to visit.

Hanna Skinner had delivered three healthy babies into the town and one stillborn. The women comforted Mrs. Dixon saying that was just God's way. Nelson and Mookie were coming to the end of another wonderful Africville summer. The workload Pa had put on Nelson was heavy but he always finished and had time to hit the tracks or shoreline with his best friend.

Maddy knew that Hope had to grab the morning paper for her father so she sat outside Hanna's from the earliest hour. Hope saw Maddy sprawled on the front porch of the shop.

"What you doing up this early?"

"I have something for you." Maddy slowly got up to her feet, reached in her smock pocket for the envelope, and handed it to Hope.

"Andre gave it to me a few days ago, but I didn't see you."

Hope smiled as she read her name on the paper. She opened it slowly and unfolded the single sheet from what she recognized as school notebook paper. It was from Vinny. She read it out loud so not to offend her friend any further.

Hope, I want you to know I am thinking about you every day. I think about you in the shadows and our dance, you sewing in the kitchen and the night on the raft. These are the thoughts that keep me sane every day.

In 4 weeks I will be getting out of this place and I will be 18, so no one can keep me away from you again. I hope you still feel the same and everything you said that night is still true. When I come home I will show you forever how much I love you. Be strong. I will be with you soon.

Love yours,
Vincent Byers

Hope folded the letter carefully and inserted it back into the envelope, placing it safely in her purse. So overjoyed was she, she grabbed Maddy and hugged her tightly.

"He is coming back to me!" she sighed.

Maddy was truly happy too. She followed Hope into the store, both exchanging conspiratorial smiles. Hanna was pleased to see the beautiful Hope happy again.

A baptism in Africville was one of the best in the Country. This was to be the last baptism of the summer — a lovely September afternoon! Cars from all over filled the parking space outside the little white church and also lined the main road all the way to the end of the town. Choir members from other churches joined in this celebration. A special preacher was brought in from one of the nearby black communities.

Sheila wore her new violet dress and her hair was done quite special. It was Hope's day. She and 20 other members of the church were to be dipped into the cool waters under the name of God and the Holy Spirit.

Hope agreed to the baptism as a way of calming her always-angered mother. But Sheila remained in a mood when it came to her only daughter.

"Get a move on it," she directed Hope to the church basement where the others were changing into their whites.

Most of the others were older than Hope and there was also Mookie Howe who looked handsome all dressed in white.

The group all filed out of the church basement and made their way down to the cove, where the wind would be less challenging. The day was sunny and crisp fresh air blew in from the north. Hope dreaded hitting that cold water; it never seemed warm on the hottest day. She looked into the crowd. There must have been over a hundred people. Women pushed their hands over their skirts to keep their dresses from blowing up in the wind. Men tried to keep their hats on. Children were fidgeting on the shore's edge.

Hope caught a look of contempt glaring from Carol Ann in the crowd. She saw Hanna Skinner holding on to Dr. Kelsie's arm for support.

The choir started to sing. It was Mookie who took the solo and brought most to tears. Hope waited until her turn then walked quickly into the cool waters. She met with Preacher Terrance Symonds who greeted her gently.

"Are you ready?" he asked.

Hope nodded and faced the crowd as he lowered her into the water. Just before sinking into the cool water Hope thought she saw Vinny's smile from the crowd but when she came back up he was gone. The moment was peaceful and the water was actually refreshing. Hope waved to her family in the crowd and saw her mother as she started walking out of the water. Sheila was finally smiling. It pleased Hope to see her mother relaxed again and she felt content as she followed the wet trail of church members back into the basement. She had been one of the last in the water. The others had changed and made their way back into the church for the social. Hope found herself alone with a big mass of unmanageable wet hair. Throwing her Sunday dress on, Hope tried to pull her hair into a bundle and braided it into a thick plait.

She heard the door open and close; she guessed it was one of the other ladies going to the bathroom. Hope threw her whites on top of the pile on the floor and grabbed her things. She stopped dead in her tracks when she saw him in the door frame.

"Vinny?" It was a mere whisper.

A huge smile spread across her face to his as she ran into his arms.

Vinny picked her up and kissed her repeatedly.

"How did you get here? Are you staying?" she could hardly catch her breath.

"I just left, just for the day. Had to see my girl!" he smiled. "Hope, I need to know that when I do come back, you're with me." He looked serious.

Hope's head moved in agreement, her eyes filled with a deep happiness. Her heart beat faster. She wanted nothing in the world but to be with Vinny.

"I am...I am with you, always!"

Vincent smiled. "Good. I have three weeks left, then I am leaving and coming home and you and me, we will start a new life, you hear me girl, you and me!"

Hope moved back into his arms. She was the happiest ever in this moment.

"I need to get back upstairs before mama comes looking for me."

Vincent reached into his pocket and held something in his enclosed hand. Hope watched him open her hand with tenderness and slowly release the gold chain into her palm.

"For my girl." He kissed her again then watched her walk slowly to the stairs.

"Thank you. I love you." He heard her voice come from the top of the stairs.

Sheila and her family were waiting in the reception area.

"You took so long." She pulled her daughter close.

"My hair." Hope made the excuse as she greeted the friends in family.

After the baptism Sheila invited the Reverend and his wife over for Sunday supper. Everything seemed to be back to calm in the Carver household. Hope sat out on the porch with Maddy and Sally as Sheila served the dessert. The evening was lovely. She had brought out her favorite china and cooked a baked chicken dinner with trimmings. She even managed a rhubarb pie to have with a new brand of tea she purchased in the city.

Sheila showed the pastor to the door and started to clean up.

"You want me to call Hope in to help?" her husband asked whilst helping himself to another piece of dessert.

"No, she's fine."

Sheila grabbed Hope's new sweater and started towards her room. Tossing the garment on the bed, the pillow moved. Something shiny had caught Sheila's eye. Lifting the pillow she saw the delicate gold chain and the letter. Sitting on Hope's bed, she read and reread the note.

The conversation with her husband was long and emotional.

"I know you want her to stay, but I am telling you, Hope will never have the life she deserves if we keep her here. I invested a lot of time and energy into teaching her. I will not have her throw it all away!"

Winston was upset; he knew he would not win this fight and that meant he would lose his daughter. But winning one over on Sheila was not to be done; he had learned that earlier in his marriage.

"She is just a girl. She does what all young girls do." Winston wanted this conversation done with, but he knew his wife would never let this go. No one ever accused him of being a strong-willed man.

"No she is not just a girl, she is my very talented daughter and she will not be riding off into the sunset with that boy and live like..."

"Like us," Winston finished her rant.

"Yes Winston, like us." Sheila took a seat beside her husband. "I can have her on the noon train tomorrow. Sarah will keep her in Boston and help her get the training she needs to become of the best pianist from Nova Scotia. She deserves that, Winston."

Sheila refused to hear any more on the subject. She continued to make plans and started packing up Hope's belongings.

Hope came home to a quiet house. Winston sat defeated on the sofa and refused to look at her when she entered.

"Hi Daddy, you're sitting in the dark. Is everything okay?"

The silence was starting to scare Hope. Her father never talked a lot but this was different; he just sat there staring at the window.

"Where's Mama?"

Winston pointed to the staircase but said nothing. Hope walked slowly up the stairs. She could hear her mother moving around and was surprised when she realized the noise came from her own room. Slowly opening the door she saw her mother bent over her bed, shoving clothes into a case. The scene looked all wrong to her. This wasn't her mother putting clean clothes in her room or doing that little tidy she often does. This was an angry woman ramming all of Hope's belongings into an old suitcase. Her dirty, torn prom dress lay across the bed in plain view.

"Mama?" Hope's voice was soft. "Mama, what are you doing?"

Sheila didn't stop or turn to face her daughter.

"My sister, Sara, in Boston, she says you can stay with her for a while and get your training back on track."

Hope couldn't believe what she was hearing.

"Boston? I don't want to go to Boston! Why would I go to Boston?"

"She has a lovely house. You're going to like it."

Sheila moved across the room to access Hope's closet and that is when Hope saw the opened letter and her chain beside the suitcase. Hope felt a panic. She couldn't breathe. Things were out of her control.

"Mama.....Mama...no, I am not going!" she cried.

Shelia shoved more into the suitcase and closed it aggressively.

"Your father will take you to the train tomorrow. I will make you a lunch."

"Mama, no, you can't just send me away," Hope pleaded.

Hearing his daughter's cries, Winston remained in his seat, heart heavy, eyes filled.

It was a cool overcast day when Hope Carver left Africville.

Hope stood on the doorstep waiting for her father to load the two suitcases into the car. Sheila went to embrace her but the young woman stepped away and got into the car without a word. Winston looked at his wife once more hoping she would cease this crazy idea. Sheila merely stood there, stone-cold, and watched as Winston and Hope got in the car and drove slowly out of the town and the only home Hope had ever known.

The following months were quiet in the town. Many of the young folk had already gone west for work. Some moved into the city. The town consisted mostly of the elders.

CHAPTER 13

Andre had borrowed Dr. Kelsie's car and drove the hour and half out of town to pick up Vinny as they had discussed weeks earlier. It was Vinny's birthday. He was 18 now and legally a man.

Vinny was waiting in the cool October morning outside the farm-style house. The large sign read 'Home for Colored Children'.

He climbed into the Chevy and slapped five for his best man, Andre.

"Take me home," he requested with a broad smile on his face.

Andre put the radio on for a distraction. He knew the news he had to tell Vinny and knew that he was not going to take it well so he kept to small talk most of the ride.

"Your pop's having a small party for you. He even had Ms. Gina bake you a pineapple cake." Andre stared straight ahead watching the road as he spoke.

"Good, I need a good time. I need to see my people and smell the Africville air. You know folks be leaving Africville by the droves, everyday someone getting on a train. I ain't never leaving, nope not this nigga. I am putting down some roots."

Andre kept quiet, knowing where Vincent was heading.

"Going get me some land and get me a job. Got a good woman and going to make it work.

The silence spoke volumes but Vinny was too stuck in his dream to notice. They were very close to the town entrance when Vinny spoke again.

"Take me right to my girl. I don't give a damn about what her mama say, she can't do nothing about it now." Vincent lit a cigarette and smiled through the first puff of smoke.

Andre pulled the truck over on the side of Africville's main road. The old truck made many sputtering sounds before the motor shut down.

"What?" Vinny asked, confused.

Andre took a deep breath; he looked out to the water then back at his friend.

"She's gone."

The words lingered as the two men sat listening to the sound of an old engine.

"Gone..? Gone where? She wouldn't leave!" His voice changed and grew louder.

"Her mother...everyone is saying her mother had her sent away. She left about a week ago. I 'm sorry."

Vinny jumped out of the truck. Andre attempted to get out too.

"No!" Vinny shook his head and tossed his cigarette to the ground. His anger was rising every second. "I will see you at the house. I need to walk," he decided.

Andre nodded. The walk from the main road to the end of Africville was about 40 minutes. Most folks grabbed rides as they came by, but he knew Vinny needed every step of this walk to cool down.

Vincent headed up the road minutes after Andre left him. He was burning with anger. Every plan, every thought he had for the past two months now vanished. His heart was heavy. Everyone who saw Vinny walking along the road that day steered well clear of him. His mood was dark and his anger was on the verge of possible danger. He only stopped once in his walk. He stopped outside Sheila Carver's house. He stood in front of the house and lit a cigarette. Feeling his presence, Sheila walked to the window. She moved the curtain slightly to see an angry young man staring back at her. Unmoved, he stayed there for what seemed like forever.

"Do something!" Sheila pleaded with Winston.

He never got up out of his chair. Vincent stayed outside Sheila house for well over an hour. He just stood there, watching and smoking.

CHAPTER 14

The winters and summers came and went. The gypsies stopped coming. Things were quiet. It was the sixties and things were changing.

More cars drove on the still unpaved road. Most of the youth had moved on: Nelson had left school after Junior High and took a job in town, Mookie moved to Calgary where he worked as a cattle rancher. Hope remained in the States, unheard from. Winston had one day gone out for a loaf of bread and never returned to Africville.

It was January 1964, a cold and sorrowful day. Nelson received a call at his work. He rushed home. The news swept across town like wildfire. No one except Dr. Kelsie even knew Liza Carver was sick. It happened quickly. She passed in her sleep beside her husband of 25 years. The town was quiet.

Nelson prepared all the funeral arrangements. Pa sat in his chair quietly and didn't shed tears, he didn't get mad, he just sat there. He seemed smaller.

They all gathered at the house after the service. Hanna and Gina brought food, and liquor was in abundance. Every inch of Pa's house was filled people who adored Liza Carver.

"She taught all three of my boys," Fletcher Byers stated sitting at the kitchen table.

"Good many folk around here loved Miss. Liza. She was good people," Hanna said as she placed more cold cuts on the table.

"Fine woman," Irene added.

"She raised that boy into a fine young man too."

The people in the room nodded in agreement. Irene reached for one of the large bottles on the table and refreshed her empty glass. Pa entered his kitchen. Tiny Brown moved to give him his chair.

"No, you're alright. I am actually going to lie down. Nelson is in the room there if anyone is needing anything."

People nodded and the room stayed silent until he was well gone.

"That poor man!" Hanna shook her head.

"She was everything to him."

"Least he has that boy around."

Irene once again refreshed her drink.

"Don't he have another son?" Irene's voice was louder than intended.

"Hush woman," Hanna tried to stop Irene in her tracks. She knew what Irene's mouth was like, once the liquor went in, everything poured out.

"Don't hush me, old woman," Irene spat.

A stream of mumbled sighs and grumbling was heard.

"Why everyone gots to hush whenever someone wanna know something in this town? The town of secrets; ain't no one all pure like that snow out there." She pointed to the window.

The room was quiet and Irene saw her chance to be heard. She cleared her throat and tried to stand. She did a small liquor wobble before steading herself by holding the back of Fletcher's chair.

"The book on all the sinning around here would be bigger than the Bible, all the messing around and double dealing, all the boozing and womanizing. But no one ever says anything in open company, like we will be hit by a bolt of lightning if what is done in the dark is said in the light. Well I ain't scared!"

Some of the people from the living room and hall gathered around the table. Irene managed to step up onto one of the dining room chairs, her version of a soap box to gain a higher standing.

"Sit down, Irene, before you say things you can't take back, cause everyone knows about who creeps into your house at night."

Hanna's words spilled laughter into the room but only fueled Irene

"That's right...I gets mine and I don't give a damn who knows, because I know why I do what I do. It's the people who act like no one knows who need be careful. You need to ask questions...I be asking why two sisters have babies that look that much alike? No one wanna ask those questions. I ask what happened to Hope Carver? Or why dark Sam thinks that yalla baby is his?"

The crowd couldn't control the outrage and laughter.

"Or what about...?"

Irene felt a strong hand pulling her down. Making sure she didn't fall, Nelson helped her to the floor.

"Ms. Irene, this is mother's final gathering. I have your coat at the door and will walk you home." The room was silent as Nelson walked Irene out of the house and into the cold.

CHAPTER 15

The winter was harsh that year. Pa had very little to say to Nelson. They ate in silence and he narrowed his conversations only to things he needed help with in the shop. Nelson worked longer hours and dated girls in the city. As soon as an opening on the trains came, Nelson took it. Packing the little brown suitcase, he made his rounds through the town. Pa had offered to drive him to the station but Nelson said his lady friend was picking him up. The last hour they had, Pa asked if he wanted his piece of pie and, even though Nelson didn't, he took the only thing his father ever offered him in kindness.

The spring brought new things to Africville, things which were not pretty like flowers, nor sweet smelling like the sea air. The newest things in Africville were suit-wearing, briefcase-toting white men.

Rita Brown was the first to open her door to one of these suspicious men.

"Morning ma'am, my name is Reginald Thorn. I work for the city. I would like to speak with you and the owner of this here house."

Rita looked at the man for a long time. She was six months pregnant the stranger noticed as Rita opened the door wider.

Reginald Thorn was not having much luck with the residents. He reached Irene Cassidy's and was chased away by a big yellow dog. A white man named Flemming took a gardening tool and chased him off his property. Most wouldn't open their doors and some even shouted obscenities when Thorn approached.

Everyday Thorn continued. He would start at the entrance of Africville at Rita Brown's, where she lived with an elder mother and her husband, and then he would work his way up. For two months he never got past the first 10 houses, but every day he continued to knock on doors.

It was a hot morning when Thorn had taken off his suit jacket and merely sat on the doorstep of Rita's house. The door opened. A small child carried a tall glass of cold tea and set it on the step beside the sweating man. Without an exchange the child ran back into the house.

Having not gone far with his tactics, Thorn hired a man from the next province of New Brunswick. Arthur Gordon was a large, well-spoken black man. His job was simple — to talk him and Thorn into the house. Black folks trust their own was a theory that proved right for Thorn. The small fee he paid the man for his presence was quite worth it. The citizens opened their doors to a man they trusted. One house after the other, Thorn made his way through the town. He was able to sit with every neighbor and present his proposed plan. It took a year.

Meetings were held in private offices in the city and in the church for the residents. People were afraid, deals were being made. Rita Brown was the first to take an offer. It wasn't a lot of money but she moved her family to Toronto and never looked back. Others had negotiated as well. Half of the town was divided. Pa called meetings. Africville was being sold piece by piece. Everyday someone took a cheque well less than their property was worth. Some people had been threatened and bullied into making deals. The city of Halifax wanted this land and they were relentless in acquiring it.

The summer of '68 was hot. The overview of Africville had changed considerably. The playing fields were empty. Fishing boats were scattered on the rocks of the shore. Few cars drove up and down the main road. Haddy's store was opening later and closing earlier. Every other house was boarded up and the wells were covered over. The last few families standing were all elders.

Nights were cold. The coal freights had stopped passing through the town. Everything had come to a slow.

Getting frustrated with the few lingering families, the officials had tried dubious tactics, pitting neighbors against each other and offering some families considerably more and telling others no more deals and they would be run off the land with nothing.

Pa Carver was the last to settle up. He shoved the dirt money cheque in his overcoat.

In September 1968 the City of Halifax drove 43 garbage trucks into Africville and loaded up the possessions of the people. The roads were congested with pickup trucks, cars, even folks walking with belongings. Dust blew, leaving the town in a cloud of brown dust.

Dr. Kelsie had already moved his belongings out of Africville. He had bought a nice house in the south end of the city. He returned to help his neighbors. It took longer than normal to make his way up the main road. He stopped outside Hanna's shop. There was no movement — no boxes on her porch and no trunk in the driveway. Stan Kelsie pulled his Chevy over when a little figure in the road stood firm in his stance.

"Ricky?"

Ricky Flemming was Gina and Charles Flemming's oldest child. He was eight years of age. His sandy colored curls were blowing in the dust. After the Chevy came to a full stop, Ricky opened the passenger door and hopped in.

"My mom sent me to help Miss. Hanna." Ricky's voice was soft. He was trembling a bit.

Stan Kelsie knew immediately not to ask many more questions, the boy was close to tears.

"You go on get out here," the doctor suggested.

Ricky hopped out of the truck a few feet from his home as the doctor drove back to Hanna's.

He entered through the shop. Every can and bottle was still in its place on the shelves. The radio was on but no one was there. He walked into the back room, calling out to Hanna – he heard nothing. Opening the door to her bedroom, he found her on her bed dressed in her Sunday best.

"Ms. Hanna, we need to get you packed and out of here."

There was no response. Doctor Kelsie knew Hanna Skinner was never going to leave Africville. He held her hand, checked her pulse, then covered her over.

With all the commotion, very few people saw the white ambulance crawl along the dust road and take Hanna Skinner out of town.

Sheila had hired some men to help carry her things to the rented truck. She was left in the room with only her beautiful piano. After many tries the men couldn't get the instrument out through either door. Getting tired from the trying, one smart thinker ran out to the truck and returned with an axe.

"What the hell are you doing?" Sheila screamed.

The workers looked at the hysterical woman.

"Ma' am, in two days all these houses are being bulldozed to the ground." He then started hacking away at her door frame.

Sheila stood there crying — crying for her house, her abandoned husband, banished daughter, and her crumbling community. On her knees, Sheila wailed.

CHAPTER 16

Most of the citizens were being relocated to housing in the center of the city — concrete-built square homes. Some moved out of the province and a few bought properties in the city. Nothing was fair or just in this traumatic relocation.

The horrible date was set. September 30 was the demolition day. All the homes had been vacated by then. The town was empty and a metal gate had been erected and surrounded it like it was a hostage.

The bulldozers were scheduled to start at 12 noon. People from everywhere came to watch the town fall. Most of the residents lined themselves closest to their own property. Reporters and news people also positioned themselves along the gates.

At 11 a.m. a train rolled through and stopped. Two passengers disembarked a few cars away from each other. They stood behind the train until it rolled on towards the city. The male passenger looked over to the woman passenger. They exchanged knowing looks before heading in their chosen directions. Carrying the small brown suitcase, Nelson appeared at the gate where Pa had been standing staring at what was his home and business for so many years. Nelson put his hand on his father's shoulder. Pa turned and hugged his son.

"Let's get out of here. You don't need to watch this."

Pa nodded. He was a much smaller man now. He had lost lots of weight. Nelson had grown into a tall handsome man. He guided his father away from the crowds and through the parked vehicles. They left having missed the biggest news to happen in Africville.

Truck 42 was being driven by Calvin Mosher. Calvin had been driving trucks for 26 years. This was one of the most exciting demolitions: three hundred houses, shops and a church all coming down, twenty trucks waiting at the beginning of the town and twenty more lined up at the end. Calvin was starting at the end of the main road at a small house with rickety stairs and a broken porch.

Skillfully, Calvin lined his bulldozer up to face house number 79. He checked his watch. It was almost time.

Hope Carver walked fast, her city shoes sinking into the dirt. Everyone was watching the scene in front. No one saw Hope as she scurried along the fence past her own homestead. A loud crack stopped her as she stood and watched the first house tumble like it was made of straw. Hope took a deep breath and moved faster.

Five years had passed since she left Africvillle. She had not spoken a word to anyone since she left, not her mother, father, no one. She broke into a quick walk as she heard the motors start up. She could barely see Vinny's house in the distance. She knew he would be there at the gate and she could finally tell him. Her heart raced.

Calvin Mosher scrutinized his watch, waiting to the very second when all hands hit twelve. He turned the key and started his engine. When he looked up again something was wrong.

A man sitting on the porch, sitting on the rail like it was any day. Calvin cut the engine and peeked up over the cab.

"Get out of there!" he yelled.

The man lit a cigarette and remained sitting calmly.

"Nigger, I ain't gonna tell you again."

No one from behind the fence could hear but everyone saw Vinny jump from his porch up onto the front of the bulldozer. What happened next sealed the fate of Vincent Byers.

Hope reached the part of the fence in front of Vinny's but even more people had now gathered.

Something seemed to be happening. The driver was being pulled from his cab and they both fell to the ground. Hope screamed for Vinny to stop; she screamed things he couldn't hear. He couldn't hear the voice of the only woman he would ever love telling him she was there, screaming unheard words lost to the traffic of devastation.

It was hardly a fight. Vincent grabbed the driver and pushed him against the steel truck, punching and screaming. His rage was unfulfilled when the driver stopped fighting back, the distant look in his eyes and the blood seeping from his head. Vincent had pushed him into the sharp blade on the truck and he died instantly. The police and other workers were a few feet away when Vincent looked into the crowd and saw his beloved Hope crying behind the fence.

Homes toppled as the city police handcuffed Vincent Byers and put him in the patrol car. Hope stepped away from the fence to see her mother only a few feet from her, both women crying huge tears.

Hope ran into her mother's arms. "He is gone," she whispered.

Sheila nodded.

"It's all gone, baby, everything."

CHAPTER 17

Africville, July 1994

Twenty-five years later, Africville celebrated the reunion. A time for family and community to come back to the land, to feel the ground that once belonged to them, to share the memories with their children. In the end the City of Halifax did nothing with the land. It became a park. The destruction of lives and community has been a black mark on Canadian history — all to put up a park. The dump was removed, grass was laid and after many, many years a mock church was built. But once a year in the late weekend of July, all the residents and families come together to this park. They barbecue, have children's events, hold a church service but, most of all, they remember.

A photo of Hanna Skinner is kept in the church. Maddy Cassidy wheels Irene through the park. Irene has stage 2 cancer. She is looking at her last reunion. She can barely speak but the look in her eyes says she is happiest with her friends and family on her land.

Andre and his wife parade through the park with their twin boys, both university students. They stop at different sites, greeting newcomers and embracing old friends.

Pa Carver died five years after the day Africville was demolished. Truth was he died with it, just took his body a while to agree.

Nelson, his wife and four children, set up his camper. His oldest son, Nelson Jr., helps assemble the barbecue. His wife tosses out the pillow and opens the doors and windows for fresh sea air to filter the moving home.

"Now that is a nice home away from home," a voice calls from the road.

Nelson can't believe Hope Carver is walking up to his campsite.

"That ain't you?" Nelson embraces the beautiful woman and introduces her to his family. He hasn't seen Hope Carver since that horrible day. A photo of her and her mother crying outside the gate was taken by a journalist. It became one of the most famous photos in Nova Scotian history.

"Wow! Hope Carver!" He shakes his head in disbelief. "You came home, after all this time."

"You haven't met my son." Hope smiles as she looks over to where a group of young men are talking. "Get over here; meet your cousin Nelson," she yells.

Nelson`s face changed from a smitten smile to shock, surprise and bewilderment.

"Vincent Byers!" Nelson's voice booms

"No!" Hope laughs. "This is my son, Winston."

But Hope had lost Nelson's attention. Nelson has rushed over to a car that has just pulled over. Out steps Vincent Byers, a much older Vinny.

At 50, Vinny is in optimum shape. He is tall and muscular, his hair braided in corn rows. He recognizes Nelson right away. The two men embrace and laugh. Hope stands in shock as Vincent looks her way.

It would seem everyone at the park stops what they are doing. Maddy drops her plate of chicken wings on the table and starts drifting over to Nelson's side. Most of the elders look their way but no one moves. Hope stands frozen, looking at the past, her past standing there after 25 years. In her head she had worked out that he was freed but she lives one day at a time, never expecting to see him again.

Vincent was moving closer towards her. Her son, Winston, steps up quickly, blocking him.

Hope pulls him back. "It's okay," she whispers.

Stopping quite close in front of her, Vincent waits. The town waits.

"Hope?" It was the voice she remembered.

Hope throws her arms around his neck, holding him tightly. She cries.

Everyone cries.

"Daddy, why are you crying?" Nelson's daughter asks.

"Because we are home," he answers.

Someone turns up the music and everyone resumes the celebration.

CPSIA information can be obtained
at www.ICGtesting.com
Printed in the USA
LVOW04s0902021216
515399LV00010B/38/P